PEARSON
Prentice Hall
BUSINESS

power at work

the art of making things happen

Jo Owen

An imprint of Pearson Education

Harlow, England • London • New York • Boston • San Francisco • Toronto
Sydney • Tokyo • Singapore • Hong Kong • Seoul • Taipei • New Delhi
Cape Town • Madrid • Mexico City • Amsterdam • Munich • Paris • Milan

PEARSON EDUCATION LIMITED

Edinburgh Gate
Harlow CM20 2JE
Tel: +44 (0)1279 623623
Fax: +44 (0)1279 431059
Website: www.pearsoned.co.uk

First published in Great Britain in 2007

ISBN: 978-0-273-71339-5

British Library Cataloguing-in-Publication Data
A catalogue record for this book is available from the British Library

Library of Congress Cataloging-in-Publication Data
A catalog record for this book is available from the Library of Congress

10 9 8 7 6 5 4 3 2 1
11 10 09 08 07

Typeset in 9/13.5pt Stone Serif by 30
Printed by Ashford Colour Press Ltd., Gosport

The publisher's policy is to use paper manufactured from sustainable forests.

contents

acknowledgements

One of the key ideas at the heart of *Power at Work* is the idea of the network: a strong network enables you to do things far beyond your own limited resources. This discovery was put into practice in writing *Power at Work*. The book would not have been possible without the generous support and help of a wide network of people who kindly gave their time.

Over the last few years I have interviewed hundreds of people in positions of power in the public, private and voluntary sectors. In the public sector I have received kind support from the French Prime Minister's office and to the Leader of the House of Lords onwards; in the voluntary sector my colleagues at Teach First, Start Up and Future Leaders have been a constant source of inspiration. In the private sector I have been fortunate enough to work with over 80 of the best, and one or two of the worst, organisations on this planet. I have learned from them all: I hope that they got back at least as much in return.

Creating such a network has relied on a few individuals who have been powerful sponsors. Rupert Goodman at FIRST Magazine and Dr. Marshall Young at Said Business School, Oxford University, gave the financial and intellectual sponsorship for a study on Anglo-French leadership which has greatly informed this book.

The ideas in this book have been shaped by countless conversations. I am particularly grateful to Gerald Ross, Dean of Faculty at McGill University; to Anthony Willoughby for his constant inspiration; to Nigel Nicholson of London Business School for his critical insight.

No book happens without the faith and support of a publisher. Richard Stagg had the foresight to encourage this project and give it shape; Sam Jackson is a genuinely useful editor who has, hopefully, helped to make the book readable. Frances Kelly is a wonderful agent who enables an author to worry about words not contracts. And finally, I am forever grateful to my wife Hiromi who endured my ramblings and rantings about power with great patience.

Anyone who aspires to power soon learns that with great power comes great responsibility. The same is true with authors: if you find fault with anything in this book, find fault with the author and not with the wonderful network of people who have given so much positive help.

introduction

For most managers, the real competition is not in the market place. The real competition is sitting at a desk nearby. In any organisation, there is a limited amount of money, promotions and bonuses to go round. Managers compete with each other for these limited resources. This is healthy for the organisation, even if it feels unhealthy for the manager. Endless internal competition is a ruthless way of discovering where the talent is. It also enables the organisation to allocate scarce resources efficiently.

Competition between managers within organisations is natural. Organisations are set up for conflict. Each department will have its own priorities and agendas, and has to fight to make its voice heard over the competing voices of other departments.

This is the world of the real manager. It is intensely competitive. As a result it is also highly political. Standard operating procedure is that your responsibilities will exceed your resources and authority. This can be hugely frustrating. Lack of resources or authority does not excuse failure or inaction. The effective manager is expected to make things happen with and through other people. This means creating alliances, doing deals, persuading, negotiating, fire fighting, resolving conflicts and crises in addition to doing the day job. This is far from the academic ideal of rational management. This is management as managers experience it: dealing with people, power and politics to make things happen.

Organisations are set up for conflict

The challenge for managers is becoming more intense every year. Flatter organisations may be lean, but they are also mean. The old certainties of rigid hierarchies are being replaced by the ambiguity of flatness: it is easier to hide, but it is harder to shine as responsibility becomes ever more diffused. The result is that managers may have to compete with each other for resources, but they also have to collaborate to make things happen. The paradox of competition and collaboration does not make organisations any more comfortable for the effective manager.

With more and more activities being outsourced, managers find that the critical resources they require may reside in a partner organisation. The days of the organisation built like a medieval walled city are over: no longer can any organisation expect to have everything from printing, catering and cleaning to the supply chain managed in-house. If managers are lucky they will have the opportunity to manage this ambiguity. If they are unlucky, they will find themselves being outsourced, offshored, best-shored or otherwise optimised out of employment.

These changes mean that the performance bar for managers has been increasing steadily. It is no longer enough to be smart (high IQ) and nice (high EQ or emotional quotient). We can all identify smart and nice managers who languish harmlessly in the backwaters of the organisation, while managers who are neither so smart nor so nice rise to the top using their colleagues as doormats to the C-suite (CEO, CFO, COO and Chairperson). The missing element is PQ: political quotient. PQ is not about stabbing your peers in the back to gain that vital promotion. PQ is about understanding how the organisation works, and developing an ability to make things happen in a world of increasing ambiguity and responsibilities, combined with decreasing authority. This is an uncomfortable world for many managers who hanker after the certainties of the old command and control world. For other managers, ambiguity represents a huge opportunity to shape and control your own destiny.

Converting ambiguity from a challenge to an opportunity depends on building a set of core PQ skills: negotiating, persuading, selling ideas, building networks, starting and managing change, managing crises and conflicts, understanding and using the sources of power in each organisation. These skills are all learnable.

The skills and principles of PQ may be universal, but how they are applied depends on where you work. The rules of success and survival are simply different in different places. For instance, risk is the life blood of a trader in an investment bank but is like Kryptonite to a civil servant. *Power* not only outlines the skills and principles behind PQ: it also shows how you can apply them in practice in your context.

PQ in practice

PQ is about the practice of how managers really make things happen, drawn from experience of working with over 80 of the best, and one or two of the worst, organisations on the planet.

PQ shows how managers actually succeed in organisations today. Fortunately, PQ is not some mysterious pixie dust like charisma or inspiration which you either have or do not have. High PQ managers all show consistent behaviours based on a core set of skills which any manager can learn, and every successful manager must learn. These skills can be grouped into six major themes which answer the who, where, how, when, what and why questions of power.

1 Who and where: weave your web

The essence of PQ is making things happen through other people. This is an obvious truism which is missed by many thousands of deeply expert technocrats in IT, engineering, law, supply chain, sales and other functions. They advance their careers on the basis of deep technical expertise for a few years. Then they hit a plateau. Technical and IQ skills do not enable them to progress any further, and yet they remain attached to the technical success formula which has served them in the past. The young dogs can not learn the new tricks of EQ and PQ. The typical skills covered in this section are:

- Weaving your personal power web
- Assessing your power web
- Using your boss

- Where to find power
- Power web traps

2 How: earning the currency of power

Given most organisations encourage competition between functions, departments and businesses, it is tempting to see PQ as a way of fighting and defeating all your colleagues. The danger with constant fighting is that you might lose. Even if you win, you will acquire too many enemies too fast. Real PQ is subtler. It is a way of winning with and through other people. Do not fight your colleagues: use them. They will help you if they get back something in return. Some managers build and use networks instinctively. Behind those instincts are a group of identifiable and learnable skills, such as earning trust, building commitments, creating partnerships and becoming the focus of power. The typical skills covered in this section are a mixture of substance and style:

- The currency of power
- Building trust to gain power
- Creating the appearance of power
- The language of power
- Power behaviour: the partnership principle

3 When: seize the moment

There are always moments of truth, when power flows to some people and ebbs from others. You can prepare for these moments of truth, because most of them are predictable. Meetings, presentations, assignment and review time are all predictable and can be prepared for. Even if a crisis, conflict or bad news is not predictable, we can predict that these things will happen at some time. When they happen, it is too late to start preparing: you need to know in advance the sorts of tactics and strategies which you can use to turn potential tragedy into triumph. The typical skills covered in this section are:

- Striking early and seizing control
- Power meetings
- Power presentations
- Persuading and influencing people
- Overcoming resistance
- Saying "no": stopping bad ideas
- Crisis management
- Dealing with awkward people

4 What: pulling the levers of power

Some people find themselves in positions of power, but do not know how to use it. They enjoy the trappings of power like royalty in a democracy: everyone knows that it is the politicians with the PQ who wield the real power. To exercise power, you need to know what the levers of power are, and how to pull them. Control over budgets, staff, change, strategy, clients, rewards and measures all give managers the opportunity to exercise control and build their PQ. Weak managers passively administer such resources: effective managers understand how to put such resources to work well. The typical skills covered in this section are:

- Negotiating budgets and the psychological contract
- Controlling budgets
- Using budgets to make things happen
- Rewards and measures
- Staffing and structures
- Knowledge and power
- Projects and change

5 Why: use it or lose it

Power flows through organisations: it constantly shifts with people, priorities and the politics of the time. Doing nothing is not an option for managers: doing nothing means that power

To stay powerful, you have to use power

ebbs away. To stay powerful, you have to use power. Use it well, and you acquire more power. This leads to behaviour which will be familiar to most managers, but is completely absent from any training manual, textbook or theory. In using power, managers have to learn to behave unreasonably at times: being reasonable achieves nothing. Managers with strong PQ understand which battles to fight and how to fight them and how to set themselves up for success. The topics covered in this section are:

- Delusions and reality of power
- Agenda power
- Unreasonable management
- Picking your battles

the principles of power

You can acquire PQ by exercising a set of core political skills. Before delving into these skills, it is worth understanding the principles behind the practice. Understanding the nature of power and your own aptitude for it and your environment are the basic building blocks for developing your own PQ. The key elements of context are:

- The nature of power in organisations
- Assessing your personal PQ score
- Assessing your environment
- The laws of power

This context helps you understand the nature of your challenge and how you can succeed.

The nature of power in organisations

To build power, it pays to know what you are trying to build. Power in organisations comes in four main flavours:

- Formal power
- Expert power
- Agenda power
- Network power

Formal power

When people think of power in organisations, they normally think of formal power: control over budgets, staff, decisions and resources. These are extremely useful types of power to control, but focus on these sorts of power brings some problems:

- In flat, complex organisations managers never have enough formal power to fulfil all their responsibilities: anyone relying on formal sources of power will become very frustrated very fast
- Having the power is useful, but the real question for most managers is how to acquire such formal power
- Formal authority is only useful to the extent it is used fully: it's not just a matter of what you have, but how you use it

To acquire formal power you first need to use the three main types of informal power: expert power, agenda power and network power.

Expert power

Expert power is attractive but weak. When graduates start their careers, they learn a functional skill. Some become so good at it, they become trapped by it in a prison of success. Technical experts can rise one or two levels in the organisation and will always be valued for their expertise (until they are outsourced or offshored).

But the technical expert rarely rises into the ranks of real power. Middle and junior ranks of management are full of technical experts doing a great job, who are being bypassed on the career ladder by people who are less technically expert but more politically adept than them. But if you really stick to it, you may rise from the masses in the middle and transform yourself from mere expert to great guru. Like the top film stars and top sports stars, this is the wish of many and the achievement of few. Like film stars and sports stars, the technical expert may be widely admired but lacks any real power. Fame and power are different destinations.

Agenda power

Strong form personal power comes from creating an agenda which commands attention across the organisation: at all levels and in all departments. With a strong agenda, a manager can start to gain visibility, build a network of influence and support and earn the right to move onto even greater responsibilities in the future. Having an agenda means having and taking control in all situations, from routine meetings to exceptional crises. If you do not control your destiny, someone else will.

If you do not control your destiny, someone else will

Network power

Network power is the strongest form of power which a manager can acquire. In organisations where responsibility routinely exceeds authority, managers need a network of influence, support and allies to make things happen. They can not succeed by relying on their own skills or their own authority: they have to find ways of leveraging the skills and resources of the rest of the organisation. Network power is at the heart of the successful PQ manager. A successful network is both broad and strong: there is no point in knowing many people unless you can influence them and make things happen through them.

assessing your power: PQ

Take a moment to check what sort of power you already have. You will undoubtedly have some power in your organisation, otherwise you would not be able to achieve anything. But if you are like most managers, you are likely to be frustrated that you do not have enough power, or the right sorts of power. Once you know what the gaps are, you can start doing something about them.

Table 1.1 is a simplified PQ assessment tool. It ignores formal power of authority over people and budgets: that sort of power is obvious and you know how much of it you have. Formal power is also the result, not cause, of PQ: to gain formal power you first need to build your informal power or PQ. Score yourself against each of the statements in Table 1.1: ideally, get a trusted peer to do the scoring with you.

How to score the PQ assessment tool

Expert power score

Sum up your scores for questions 1, 4, 7, 10 and 13.

Scores over 20: You are clearly a valued expert in your own field. This makes you a very useful member of your organisation. It is also a huge trap for you. Great technicians often find it tough to escape the technician tag and you may become a "guru in a box". This is clearly a viable and relatively safe career choice, but it is not the route to power.

Scores 15–20: You have probably demonstrated competence in your chosen trade. This gives you a base from which to build your network, agenda and your political power: you are not in danger of falling into the "guru in a box" trap.

Table 1.1 Political quotient (PQ) assessment tool

	1 Disagree strongly	**2 Disagree Slightly**	**3 Half-way**	**4 Agree Slightly**	**5 Agree strongly**
1 My peers ask me for advice in my area of expertise					
2 I know the top three agenda items for my boss this year					
3 I can rely on a wide range of peers for support					
4 I am widely regarded as an expert in my field					
5 I know the top three agenda items for my boss's boss this year					
6 I know about the birthdays, families, past times of my peers					
7 I can solve the most challenging problems my staff face					
8 My work is critical to the promotion/ bonus prospects of my boss					
9 My peers regularly ask for advice and coaching outside my area of expertise					
10 I get assigned the toughest tasks in my area of expertise					
11 My boss's boss actively supports my work					

Table 1.1 Continued

	1 Disagree strongly	2 Disagree Slightly	3 Half-way	4 Agree Slightly	5 Agree strongly
12 I understand my peers' agendas and can align my needs with theirs					
13 I get to speak externally (clients, conferences) in my area of expertise					
14 I understand my boss's working style and adapt to it successfully					
15 I understand my peers' working styles and adapt to them successfully					

Scores under 15: You are either still learning your trade, or you have progressed so far that technical expertise is not your critical survival tool. With relatively modest technical skills, your political skills and an ability to make things happen are essential to your continued success.

Agenda power score

Sum up your scores for questions 2, 5, 8, 11 and 14.

Scores over 20: You are working on a high visibility and high impact agenda which will accelerate your career: you will succeed fast or you will fail fast. You are on the political high road with a power agenda.

Scores 15–20: You are hunting with the pack. Along with many of your peers you are working on relevant and worthwhile initiatives. Your challenge is how to stand out from the pack: you need to develop a claim to fame which will be recognised in the wider organisation.

Scores under 15: You probably lack visibility, power and possibly relevance to the wider organisation. Your boss may be delegating only routine rubbish to you. You are therefore largely dispensable to the organisation. Seek a better agenda to support your boss on more important items, or seek a new boss.

Network power score

Sum up your scores for questions 3, 6, 9, 12 and 15.

Scores over 20: Your real name may be Machiavelli. You are naturally a good networker; you build alliances and the chances are that you are able to get things done without relying on formal authority.

Score 15–20: You are surviving in a complex and ambiguous world. To progress and really make things happen, you will need to build your power network at all levels of the organisation.

Scores under 15: I wrote this book for you. You may well be diligent, hard working and smart. This makes you ideal fodder to be exploited by more political bosses and peers who will use your goodwill and expertise to advance their careers. You need more balanced relationships with your peers: more take for what you give.

assessing your environment

Every organisation is political. Some are more political than others. The more political organisations are marked by greater ambiguity, opportunity and risk for managers. Less intensely political organisations stick more closely to formal, predictable and transparent rules and procedures: the informal rules of survival are similar to the informal rules of success.

more political organisations are marked by greater ambiguity, opportunity and risk for managers

As with organisations, so with hierarchy. The rules of survival and success are often fairly obvious at lower levels of the organisation. A new salesperson may have a tough sales target, but it is obvious what success looks like. The more senior you become, the less obvious the rules of survival and success become. Ambiguity, opportunity and risk all rise. The formal and informal rules of the game part way.

The test in Table 1.2 will indicate how overtly political your environment is. The challenge is then to match your style to your environment. Answer the 20 questions in Table 1.2: you will quickly see that people in different parts of the same organisation, and with different bosses, will experience different levels of political intensity. Once you have completed your answers, go to the Appendix, page 162, for the scoring guide. You will then be able to find a score out of 100 for the political intensity of your environment.

The median score from this tool is 70: this represents a typical level of political intensity. If you score below this you are in a relatively apolitical organisation. Anything below 55 is unusual: you may want to check whether you really understand the politics that are swirling around you, or whether you are being naïve.

The test below will indicate how overtly political your environment is. The challenge is then to match your style to your environment. Answer the 20 questions below: you will quickly see that people in different parts of the same organisation, and with different bosses, will experience different levels of political intensity. Once you have completed your answers, go to p. 162 for the scoring guide. You will then be able to find a score out of 100 for the political intensity of your environment.

Table 1.2 Political environment (PE) assessment tool

	1 Disagree strongly	**2 Disagree slightly**	**3 Half-way**	**4 Agree slightly**	**5 Agree strongly**
1 My responsibility exceeds my authority					
2 Resources are allocated strategically and rationally					
3 You get the resources you negotiate					
4 My goals for this year are clear					
5 My goals remain unchanged over the year					
6 The promotion process is fair, rational and transparent					
7 You need strong sponsorship to get promoted					
8 Assignments balance the needs of the organisation and the individual					
9 You get the assignment you negotiate					

Table 1.2 Continued

	1 Disagree strongly	2 Disagree slightly	3 Half-way	4 Agree slightly	5 Agree strongly
10 There are not enough promotions to go round					
11 There are not enough bonuses to go round fairly					
12 My boss frequently praises the team					
13 Mistakes are used to help people learn and develop					
14 Sort problems out before the boss finds out					
15 The real rules of survival and success are not written down					
16 We operate an up or out policy					
17 This is a highly ethical and moral organisation					
18 Honesty is highly valued					
19 Politically astute people get promoted first					
20 I trust my boss completely					

Scores above 80 are typical of the more intensely political environment: middle and senior management in professional service firms or large and complicated matrix organisations will often score high.

assessing your position on the political quotient/ political environment grid

The PQ assessment tool and the PE assessment tool now enable you to assess your overall position in your context. Plot your position on the grid in Table 1.3. Any score above 70 in the PE assessment tool is high: plot your score in one of the right-hand boxes. Next, find your total from your network power score and agenda power score in the PQ assessment tool. Any score over 30 marks you out as a relatively high PQ manager: plot your position in one of the two upper boxes. Clearly, the division between high and low is abrupt: you may well find that you are closer to the middle than to the edges of the grid.

You can succeed or fail wherever you are on this matrix: the nature of failure or success depends on where you are. Even the lambs to the slaughter can succeed, provided they do not aspire to positions of power. If they are happy being great technicians in IT, HR, accounting or elsewhere, they will be safe and they will be valued by the organisation. They are more likely to survive shake-outs than the power players who live by power and die by power.

The real rules of success and survival are never written down

Foxes are the opposite of the lambs to the slaughter. They are strong political operators in relatively low politics organisations: this means that foxes enjoy accelerated careers: they succeed fast or they fail fast. They have to play politics well and discreetly. Being overtly political becomes a career limiting move in this sort of organisation.

The sheep and the sharks are suited to their respective environments. Vast herds of sheep exist at more junior management levels in machine bureaucracies: central government, large utility compa-

Table 1.3 Political quotient/political environment grid

Political quotient		Low politics environment	High politics environment
50	**High PQ manager**	*The fox* – makes things happen, to advantage of self and organisation – moves fast, but gains enemies fast – feared and admired within organisation	*Swimming with sharks* – uses ambiguity and uncertainty to advantage – works formal and informal systems well – manages both substance and style: appearance and performance
30 / 10	**Low PQ manager**	*The sheep* – guided by twin stars of fairness and efficiency – wait your turn, don't mess up – process as important as outcome	*Lambs to the slaughter* – belief in doing a good job first – often technocrats who are squeezed out of line positions – can be frustrated on the sidelines
		20	70 — 100

Political environment

nies and life insurance companies are sheep farms in management terms. The sheep face a challenge as they rise: they have to make a remarkable and unusual transformation into becoming a fox or a shark: this goes against received evolutionary theory. But the sheep will find that as they become more senior, the politics, ambiguity, uncertainty, risk and opportunity all rise. They have to learn a new way of operating if they are to survive, let alone succeed.

Sharks are becoming more common as the workplace becomes more sophisticated. The old certainties and rigidities of the functional hierarchy where everyone waited their turn to be promoted are becoming increasingly uncommon. Instead, the workplace is full of opportunity, risk and uncertainty. The real rules of survival and success are never written down: you have to decode them from the behaviour of colleagues and bosses. Learning the laws of power is no longer an optional extra for ambitious individuals: in many organisations understanding power is becoming the only way to be effective and to make things happen.

the ten laws of power

Behind the core skills of PQ there are some behaviours which we saw high PQ managers display repeatedly. They were like default settings in their mindset. The more uncertain, ambiguous and challenging the situation became, the more likely they were to show these behaviours. These themes are so consistent in high PQ managers that they can be described as the ten laws of power. The ten laws of building power are:

1. Take control
2. Build your network
3. Act the part
4. Strike early
5. Pick your battles
6. Be (selectively) unreasonable
7. Go where the power is
8. Embrace ambiguity
9. Focus on outcomes
10. Use it or lose it

These laws are described briefly below.

1 Take control

Do not wait until you are CEO before taking control. High PQ managers take some control at any level of the organisation. Taking control is as simple as having a clear agenda and acting on it. Your agenda can be told as a story in three parts:

- This is where we are
- This is where we are going
- This is how we will get there

By taking control with a clear agenda, you create clarity, focus and purpose for yourself and your colleagues. Even if they disagree with your agenda, at least the discussion will be focused on your agenda and not on theirs. Taking control is especially important in crises and conflicts where there is ambiguity and risk. Many people will hide: the high PQ manager will see this as an opportunity to make a mark.

2 Build your network

You will not control all the resources to deliver the results you have to deliver. You will rely on colleagues and contractors. Occasionally you can coerce them into doing something for you on the basis of saying, "This is what the big bad boss demands..." Usually, you will get more out of your network if they support you. Building support means building trust: you need to develop mutual understanding (shared values) and mutual respect (delivering on commitments). Building trust is different from building friendships: trust is the core of professional relationships, friendship is the core of personal relationships.

3 Act the part

If you want to look like and act like a junior manager, your wish will be granted: you will stay a junior manager. You will not be taken seriously. Observe how people dress, talk and behave two levels above you. If there is a big gap between their behaviour and yours, think about changing. This can be as shallow as dressing the way they dress: you should not be judged on how you look, but you will be. But it is also more subtle. At senior levels, executives do not persuade each other with 300 page PowerPoint® presentations. They sit and talk through the issues clearly. If you give the long presentation, you position yourself as a junior executive and you will be judged that way. If you act as the partner and colleague of senior executives, helping them progress their agenda, you are more likely to be treated as a partner. This is the partnership principle: act as a partner to senior executives, not as their servant (unless you want to be treated as a servant).

4 Strike early

By acting pre-emptively, high PQ managers take control and set the agenda on their terms. Wherever there is uncertainty, ambiguity or doubt, the high PQ manager uses this to take control while others wait nervously on the sidelines. Acting early takes courage. A few examples of where acting early helps the PQ manager:

- Negotiating budgets: agree the broad objectives early, before the framework is dictated to you. Once the framework is set, 80% of your room to manoeuvre has been lost
- Managing crises: the earlier a crisis is sorted out, the less severe it is. And if you have the plan for sorting it out, you retain control. Acting late means the crisis gets worse and you risk losing control
- Getting the right assignment. Waiting for HR to advertise a position is too late. Your network should alert you to what opportunities are coming up: make sure you have positioned yourself with the right line managers to be placed where you want
- Managing meetings and overcoming resistance. Never use a meeting to make a decision. By the time an agenda item of yours goes to a meeting you should know that the decision will be positive. You should have pre-empted all the potential opposition in private meetings before the formal decision making meeting

5 Pick your battles

Battles are endemic to organisational life. As long as there are not enough resources, bonuses and promotions to go around there will be conflict. The high PQ manager will fight, but only where necessary. The three golden rules of knowing when to fight are:

- Only fight when there is a prize worth fighting for
- Only fight when you know you will win
- Only fight when there is no other way of achieving your goal

Most corporate battles fail at least one of these three rules.

6 Be (selectively) unreasonable

Any reasonable manager will understand why achieving the cost cuts, the revenue targets, the profit goal and the new market launch in record time against entrenched competition is not possible. When you accept excuses, you accept failure. High PQ managers know when and how to stretch people to achieve things they did not think were possible. By stretching people, they learn and develop. By stretching people, the organisation grows and develops. There are some managers who take this to an extreme: they are always unreasonable and they do not stretch people, they break people. Macho management is fashionable in some circles: it trades off short term gains for the long term destruction of human and economic capital. High PQ managers know how to build long term performance by being unreasonable selectively.

When you accept excuses, you accept failure

7 Go where the power is

Every organisation has centres of power. It is usually a function or a business unit which drives the rest of the organisation and where all the future leaders of the organisation are groomed. This is where the key decisions and appointments are made. That is where you need to be. Life in the power centre is often demanding and uncomfortable: it is also where you can best build your network, influence events and accelerate your career.

8 Embrace ambiguity

Ambiguity represents both risk and opportunity. Where there is ambiguity, there is often a vacuum waiting to be filled by the high PQ manager. Ambiguity arises wherever there is an uncertain agenda which no one yet owns, for instance:

- How shall we organise the offsite team meeting?
- How shall we respond to this new competitive move?
- Who should work on this new project?
- How can we deal with this crisis?

The high PQ manager will move early and take control of selected opportunities. This leaves other managers responding to the high PQ manager's agenda and playing a supporting role. The high PQ manager stands out as someone who is positive and action focused: they then need to deliver success if they are to gain any credit. The very high PQ manager then conspicuously shares the credit with everyone else, ensuring gratitude and support from others while reinforcing the fact that they were in control: a bit part player is not in a position to hand out credits.

9 Focus on outcomes

Focus on outcomes should be obvious. But it is not. Many managers find it safer to focus on analysis, processes, procedures and problems. Focus on outcomes helps managers achieve results, take control, look positive and deal with conflict. Outcome focus starts with asking the right questions:

- Meetings: what do I want to achieve from this meeting (regardless of the formal agenda)?
- Conflict with another department: what is the result I want to achieve and is it worth fighting for?
- Crises and setbacks: what is the outcome we need? Not who is to blame and what went wrong?

Outcome focus helps the high PQ manager look positive and active, while others look relatively passive or negative as they focus on analysis and problems. Outcome focus also minimises unnecessary conflicts: instead of playing the blame game and arguing over what went wrong, outcome focus is forward looking and drives to action.

10 Use it or lose it

Once you have got your hands on the levers of power, use them. The better you use them, the more formal power you will acquire. Use them poorly, you will lose formal power and possibly lose your job. Many executives acquire formal power and then play safe: they essentially continue with the same strategy, budget and performance as before, plus or minus a bit. The best predictor of next year's budget, strategy and performance is this year's budget, strategy and performance. Playing safe is legitimate if your only goal is survival. If you want to succeed, you have to make a difference. Try to answer one simple question: "What will be different as a result of my performance in this role?" Many CEOs fail this test: try to remember what a CEO of your organisation from ten years ago achieved. What will your legacy be and how will you be remembered? You will not be remembered, nor will you remember, a year in which you beat the revised budget by 6%. Use power to make a real difference.

who and where: weave your web

Success in organisations depends on weaving a web of power and influence. You can not do everything yourself. You need the right allies in the right places to make things happen for you. The first task is to know who the right people are and where to find them. The core skills to build are:

- Weaving your personal power web: knowing which allies you need
- Assessing your power web
- Using your boss
- Where to find the power hot spots in your organisation
- Avoiding the traps of the power web

weaving your personal web of power

No manager can succeed alone. At the heart of the manager's job is the ability to get things done through other people. You have to weave a web of alliances, influence and power which cuts right across the traditional silos of the organisation.

Weak managers depend on the authority of their boss. Your boss is essential to success, but if you depend on your boss alone, you become a slave. Academia is full of slaves who are also known as PhD students. They totally depend on their professor for their future career, and land up doing all the worst jobs (like teaching undergraduates and marking papers) for a pittance of a salary. In between doing this, they are allowed to do all the research for which the professor will be able to claim the credit in a scholarly journal.

if you depend on your boss alone, you become a slave

PQ demands that you weave a web of power and support beyond your immediate boss. This serves two functions:

- The power web creates career options and insurance for you
- The power web enables you to make things happen across the organisation

Here, we will look at the sorts of people you need as part of your power web. The next section will look at how you can attract these people into your web.

There are six types of people, beyond your boss, who you need in your web:

- Godfather
- Gatekeepers

- Technicians
- Coaches
- Influencers
- Contributors

Notable by its absence from this list is your boss. There are two reasons for this:

- The power web is about building the informal networks of power and support which go beyond the formal systems of the organisation
- The boss is sufficiently important to merit a separate section. Most bosses would by happy to agree with this definition of their importance

Godfather

Think of the godfather as the mafia don. This is the boss who has the authority and power to make things happen. Ideally, you will know at least a couple of executives who are at least two levels above you. These relationships are always informal and exist outside the standard power structure. Power dons like to know what is going on, like to have a wide group of potential allies to call on and like to feel that they are valued in their own right: you may be only a power pawn, but you are still attractive to the power dons.

The fairy godfather

I was Mr. Flash and sitting in the next cubicle was Mr. Fairy. We were both in brand management: I was looking after Flash and my colleague was looking after Fairy Toilet Soap. One day, the biggest Godfather of them all came down for an informal walk around. It was our CEO. It was rather like a visit by royalty. He would ask each person how things were going and he would get a confused and panicked reply (in my case at least) assuring him that everything was going fine, just fine, thank you.

He asked Mr. Fairy how things were going. Immediately, Mr. Fairy told him how excited he was about a new promotional idea, and would the CEO like to give some advice. The CEO had been Mr. Fairy himself many years ago, so was delighted to get involved again. Ten minutes later the current Mr. Fairy had achieved two things which I had missed:

- *He had made a great impression on the Godfather, who was now his Fairy Godfather*
- *He had saved himself about six weeks' political slog by getting the CEO to back his new idea: all the other departments fell in line as soon as they realised that the CEO was supporting the idea*

Ever since, I have always been ready for the chance conversation with key executives. The principles are easy: have an agenda which you are ready to share and work to the style of the person you bump into. In an informal encounter, this normally means acting informal and relaxed (even if you do not feel it) and asking for advice rather than pushing some idea aggressively.

Gatekeepers

Gatekeepers are people who can give you access to the real power barons. Secretaries are an obvious example. Most of them are poorly treated: they are either ignored, harassed or condescended to. By treating them as professionals (which they are) and as human beings (which they are) you are likely to find them mysteriously able to open their baron's diary for you when you need it. Some mid level executives will pose as gatekeepers. They will promise you access to the power don, provided that they really understand what you need. If you agree to this, you have just surrendered all control. This sort of gatekeeper will keep on demanding more and more from you, and may never even be able to deliver the access promised anyway. Be kind to such posers, but ignore them. If they are blocking you, quietly do an end run around them: engineer a chance meeting with the don in the corridor, at a conference, in the canteen and make the gatekeeper irrelevant.

Technicians

Technicians abound in organisations. These are the people who like to say "no" because that is the only power they have. They can not authorise what you are doing, but they can stop it. These people will include legal, health and safety, brand police, HR, technology and finance employees. They will say no if:

- Your idea transgresses any of their precious standards, rules and procedures
- Your idea carries any sort of risk which may eventually embarrass them
- They do not like you or your boss
- They have a competing agenda which they need or want to promote

It pays to get these people on your side early, however painful it may be. You know that when the CEO sees some numbers, he or she will ask the CFO if they make sense. If the CFO says no, you are doomed. If you already have the CFO on your side, the discussion quickly comes to a painless conclusion. Be nice to the technicians, respect their professional concerns, find out what is on their agenda and make sure you do not compete with it too overtly.

Coaches

In power terms a coach is not some external advisor with a dubious coaching qualification. A good coach is a well placed, internal executive with real seniority on whom you can rely for insight and advice on how to handle things. Surprisingly, these people exist. Senior executives are often flattered to be asked for counsel and advice; they like having other (often younger) executives around them who can tell them what is really going on and can act as their eyes, ears and occasionally as a spare pair of hands. It is a wholly informal relationship which exists outside the formal power structure. They are often particularly valuable in providing early warning of storms coming, and of attractive or deadly assignments which may be looming.

Influencers

Influencers lurk in the background and are easily overlooked. Often they carry little formal power, which makes them all the more trusted by key players in your web. With little formal power, they are not seen to be prejudiced or competing. Often, these are long time employees who have seen everything and know everyone, but they have been quietly sidelined into some sort of staff role: planning, ombudsman, development, special projects are the sorts of titles they may well have. Consultants are also classic influencers: they may well be hired by the CEO and be trusted simply because they are above the immediate day to day political battles of the organisation. It is easy to be wary of consultants: understand their agenda and quietly get to know them and coopt them onto your agenda. If influencers are speaking up for you, that will ease the way for you.

Contributors

Contributors are all the people whose active help you need, over whom you have no formal control. In a matrix organisation, this is likely to be a wide range of your peers and colleagues. The chances are that they are under as much pressure as you are, so this is where you learn to do deals. You need to find ways of making it easy for them to work with you: make sure your requests are focused and timely. Don't waste their time with trivia, last minute panics or ill thought through requests. You will not just waste their time: you will be wasting your personal equity and credibility. Be ready to reciprocate, if you can: give them help when they need it. Be generous in recognising their great contribution (even if it was a very modest contribution): send emails to them thanking them and copy their boss in on the email.

The keeper of the keys to power

Caroline joined the advertising agency as an account executive. Her job was to arbitrate between the highly demanding and emotional creative types on one side, and highly demanding and rational (occasionally) client types on the other side. She realised that she needed to find out how things really worked in the organisation, and started to get to know the big power barons in the agency. The power barons were easy to spot: loud clothes, loud voices and loud opinions.

The real challenge was to get stuff done. There was always too much work for the capacity available: getting time from the creatives, the production department, the design and research groups was a nightmare. The agency realised that if each power baron browbeat each department into putting their own work ahead of everyone else's, it would be a zero sum game. So they created the role of traffic master to schedule work on a more rational basis. Instead of shouting at many different departments, the power barons shouted only at the traffic master. It was the most thankless job in the agency: everyone thought that their own work should come first, and the traffic master had to prioritise conflicting and unreasonable demands at all times of day and night.

Caroline met the traffic master on a bad day. Everyone had been shouting at him. She sat down, chatted and commiserated with him. As a favour, the traffic master put some work through for her fast. She thanked him, and got to know more about his life, his hopes and fears. She was the only person who talked with him rather than shouting at him. Mysteriously, Caroline's work always seemed to land up getting done faster than anyone else's. Caroline discovered that real power lay not with the power barons, but with the traffic master: he was the gatekeeper to the rest of the organisation. He opened the gate for her willingly; he only grudgingly opened it for the barons who thought they were powerful.

power often exists outside the formal power structure

Caroline discovered that power often exists outside the formal power structure.

assessing your power web

Power webs grow and shift over time. Each one is personal: your network of power will be unique because you have unique needs in the organisation. A simple way of assessing your needs and progress is to draw your own power web. A power web looks like Figure 2.1.

You are at the centre of the power web. You want to be surrounded by the six sources of power you need to make things happen in your organisation. There are two considerations:

- How much power each person has relative to your needs: the more powerful they are to you, the further your web spreads. Place the most powerful and valuable people on the outside ring
- How strongly each person in the web supports you: give each person a score from 1 (not at all a supporter) to 5 (very strong supporter)

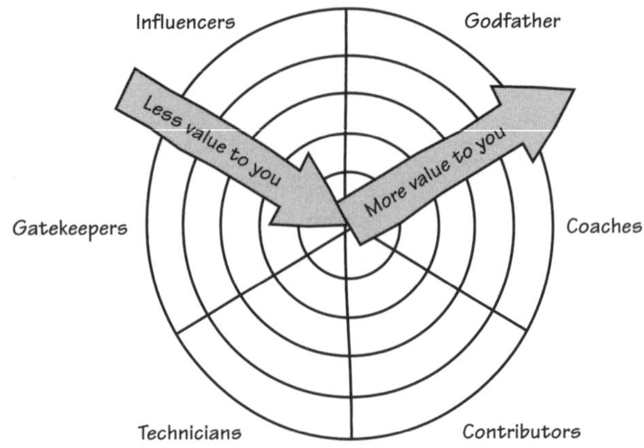

Figure 2.1 The power web

Figure 2.2 is an example from a senior executive who moved organisations. Sandy had been very successful and had been head hunted to join a rival organisation. At the end of the first day she reflected on her position, which looked like this:

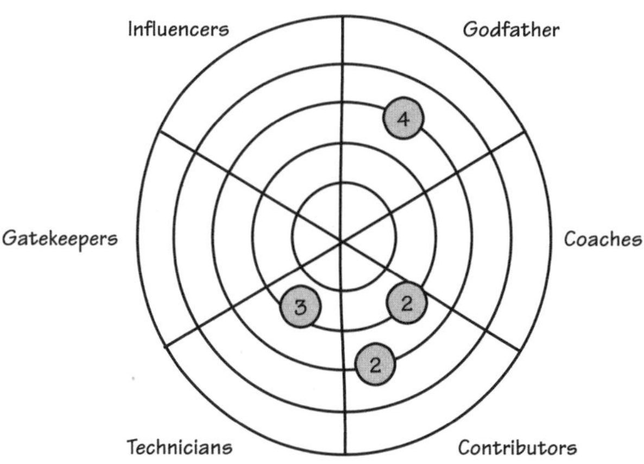

Figure 2.2 The weak power web: day one

This was a disaster. She had no real power in her new organisation. She assessed her position as follows:

Sponsor: The senior executive who championed her cause was her main ally and sponsor (scored 4 in the sponsor role). She realised that he was not as powerful as she had been led to believe in the interview process. At best, his influence in the executive team was middling, so she put him in the middle ring.

Contributors: Sandy inherited a couple of staff members whom she controlled: she was not sure they were very effective (so they were towards the centre of the web) and they were clearly nervous about their new boss. They could hardly be called allies yet: she scored them 2 at best.

Technicians: Sandy knew none of the critical people in finance, IT, operations, planning or elsewhere. She only knew the HR people who had managed her transition. They were mild supporters (she scored them a 3) and they were clearly not hugely relevant to her future needs, so she put them towards the centre of the web.

Sandy reviewed her power web. It was a shock. In her old organisation she had been very effective because she knew all the power brokers, had formed alliances with them and as a result could make things happen. She realised that she was going to be relatively ineffective in her new role until she could build an effective power web.

Over the course of the next year, she assiduously cultivated her power network and soon became known as someone who made things happen. At the end of the year, she decided to review her power web. She had some difficulty in cutting her web down to the top twenty executives she needed to deal with. Figure 2.3 was the result.

The changes were dramatic:

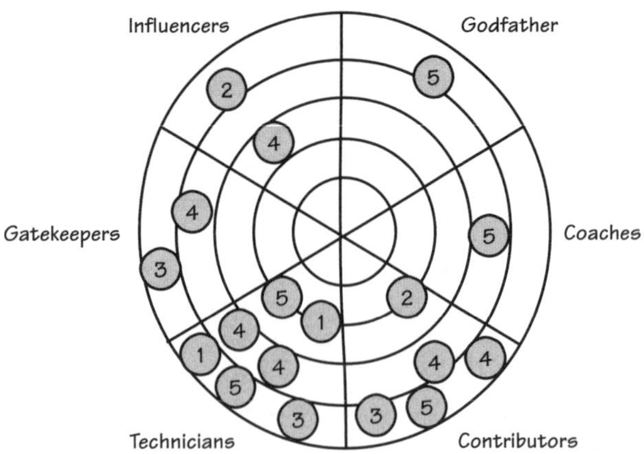

Figure 2.3 The growing power web: year end

Sponsor: Sandy got lucky. Her sponsor got promoted and clearly expanded his influence in the executive team, and she was able to strengthen her alliance with him. He had consistently helped her in political battles, and she had consistently delivered against expectations. She scored him a 5 for being a strong supporter, and put him in a power position towards the edge of the web. She needed to take no further action with regard to her sponsor.

Coaches. Sandy found a long time executive who had been quietly moved out of a P&L role to become head of planning. Most middle rank executives saw him as part of the corporate police that got in the way. But Sandy realised that he had regular access to the CEO; he was trusted by senior executives because he was above the day to day politics and because of his deep knowledge of the business. In planning, he also heard of new initiatives very early. He became an invaluable source of advice, support and information: the coach was so pleased to be so visibly valued by another executive that he was delighted to give this support.

Contributors: Sandy moved quickly to build her team. She removed one of her original staff members. Her doubts about the other were reciprocated by the staff member: she scored him a 2. The rest of the team was pretty good and they supported her: she scored them highly with the exception of one new team member who needed to get established.

Technicians: Sandy had mixed results with the staff departments. She had made an enemy of the head of legal services when she bypassed him with a major proposal which got the nod from the CEO. She scored him a 1 and put him in the power ring on the edge of the web. She needed to bring him back on board. She had also lost the brand police overboard with some negative comments about a rebranding they had been proposing. She was not too worried: there was not much the brand police could do to affect her in operations. They scored a 1, but in the weak ring at the centre of the web. She would make peace with them eventually. She had done a pretty good job of bringing the other departments on board. In particular, finance was highly supportive (scoring a 5) and very powerful (in the power ring on the outside).

Gatekeepers: The CEO's secretary was highly protective of his time: Sandy put her at the edge of the power ring. But the secretary was also highly professional: she seemed to show no favours to anyone. Sandy wondered if it was worth investing more time with her or not. She scored her a 3 at most.

Influencers: Sandy had taken care to meet various union officials informally, even although there were no formal negotiations happening. The senior official had built his reputation on the basis of thirty years of confrontation with management: she scored him a 2 and he remained dangerously powerful. Fortunately, she got to know some of the other, less powerful, officials who were much more supportive of her: she scored them a 4 for their support.

Reviewing the power web, it became obvious that Sandy had made huge progress: her personal power had grown and her value to the organisation had grown as well. She also saw where she needed to invest more time in strengthening her web. She needed to do more for a few of the key people in staff departments. She realised the brand people could become a real problem: she was being lined up to lead a market facing programme and would need their support. The power web changes each time you change role or take on a new responsibility.

using your boss

The most important person in your power web is your boss. This is an unequal relationship in even the most democratic organisation. Put simply, it is more important for you to please your boss than it is for your boss to please you.

The first step is to make peace with the boss: the boss is the fountain of formal power over your bonus, promotions and assignments. Having a strong and supportive boss is a short cut to power: you can rise on the back of your boss who will be keen to keep a known and trusted team together as he or she rises through the organisation. If you have a very good boss, this can be a highly effective career strategy. There are three risks with this career strategy:

it is more important for you to please your boss than it is for your boss to please you

- The boss may not succeed
- Managers who become accustomed to being a supporting actor often find it hard to become a leading actor. They become totally dependent on their boss succeeding and staying within the organisation.
- To remain useful to a power boss, you have to make things happen by building your power network across the organisation: you still need to weave a power web

A successful relationship with the boss is based on three fundamentals:

- Performance
- Style
- Trust

Performance speaks for itself. Always deliver and avoid surprises. If there is a problem, don't hide it. Either fix it fast, or get help fast. If you do not perform, expect either to get fired or, more likely, offloaded onto another unsuspecting manager. If you are a really nice person, you simply make the process of dumping you slightly more painful for the boss, but you still get dumped eventually.

Style counts. Each boss is different. In this unequal relationship, if you do not like the style of the boss you are the one with the problem. Either you adapt and get along with the boss, or you get out. How to adapt to different styles of bosses and colleagues is covered more fully later on.

Trust is at the heart of all good relationships, from marriage through to surviving your boss and your colleagues. If there is no trust, there is no relationship. Clearly, good performance helps drive trust up. But performance is not enough. Unswerving loyalty helps as well. Look carefully at which politicians get promoted: competence and personal morality are helpful, but loyalty is the strongest currency of all. Politicians with at best modest competence and morality get preferred over more competent politicians whose loyalty is in doubt. More on how to build trust is covered in section 3.

Trust is a two way street. You have to be able to trust your boss as much as your boss trusts you. If you do not trust your boss to act in your best interests, you are unlikely to enjoy the relationship. This is the point at which you need to look at your power web (see above). If you have a good power web, you should have identified and avoided the nightmare boss: even if you get unlucky, the power web will help you identify diplomatic exit routes from your nightmare. With a weak power web, you are stuck with an uncomfortable choice:

- Sweat it out. The corporate carousel turns steadily and no boss lasts forever: on average, less than two years. You can learn much, even negative lessons, from any boss. And then you can hope to get lucky in the next assignment process. But hope is not a method and luck is not a strategy: you need to control your destiny or someone else will

- Find the exit door. The exit door may lead to an internal reassignment (which requires working the power web) or it may be in a new organisation (where you will have no power web at all to start with)

Falling out with your boss in style

He was a good Marketing Director with one unfortunate habit. He was always in a rush, so he always walked through doors before his CEO. Harry, the CEO, valued his status and wanted to go first: boys will be boys, especially in the C-suite. Harry started ranting to me about the director's behaviour. 'But', I protested on the director's part, 'he's useful to you: he speaks seven languages.'

Harry exploded with rage: 'I'd rather have someone who is smart in one language than dumb in seven!' At this point, I made the mistake of laughing: he had just given every speaker of a single language the perfect riposte to the smugness of accomplished linguists. Harry took my laughter as confirmation that he should fire the Marketing Director.

Two hours later I was walking back towards Harry's office and I met the Marketing Director coming in the opposite direction. He was shouting and swearing (in several languages). He was also accompanied by four security guards: one holding each limb as they carried him off the premises. That was the last time I saw him and the first time I really appreciated the power of style.

where to find power

Willy Sutton, the American bank robber, was asked why he robbed banks. "Because that is where the money is", he replied. If you want money, go where the money is. If you want fame, go where the fame is. If you want power, go where the power is.

Power clearly resides in the C-suite. Knowing this does not mean you can wander in and take power. Everyone else is attracted to the same source of power like moths are attracted to a light: some get too close and get burned as a result. Look more carefully at the people in the C-suite and especially at the power barons just beneath the C-suite. The power barons will be running countries, business units or industry groups of some sort. Find out where they all come from. In many organisations, they will all come from the same function or country. These are the power factories which produce the future leadership talent and which drive the company today, even if the other functions do not want to admit it.

There are some obvious consequences of this. Most organisations favour nationals from their own country. The exceptions are clear (at Sony and Nissan for example). The whole point is that they are exceptions. The rule is that home country nationals rule. If you join an organisation which is foreign to you, the odds will be stacked against you. The critical decisions over Toyota's future are not made in England.

Just as some countries are power factories, so are some functions. Not all functions are equal. At Procter & Gamble you can have a long and safe career in HR, manufacturing, sales or finance. But marketing clearly rules the organisation: most of the leadership comes from marketing and most of the critical decisions are driven by marketing. That is where the power is.

If you want to make things happen and advance your career, it makes sense to be in the power factory. The one problem with this strategy is that all the best and brightest people are doing the same thing. You may be a star, but it is hard to shine above the others when you are in the middle of a galaxy of talent. So at some point, it makes sense to take a risk and go somewhere you can shine. If there is an early opportunity to go and run a small business, or a country, away from the power factory, take it. Everyone has to learn what it is like to take final responsibility and to run something. You gain both experience and credibility from such responsibility.

When you take on a posting in a far flung part of the empire, there are a few golden rules:

- Never believe any promises made about jobs being held open for you when you return. By the time you return, the position will have been restructured and you will have new bosses with no interest in what past bosses may or may not have promised
- Work your network hard. Find excuses to stay in touch with the power factory and buy as many round the world tickets as needed to make sure they do not forget your face. Your network will alert you to the evolving politics and what career opportunities might be available on your return
- Stake your claim to fame. The chances are that most people will not really understand how well or poorly you are doing, beyond seeing what the financial results look like. Make sure that everyone understands the scale of the challenge you faced and how you met the challenge: tell a story which brings the numbers to life. You will be remembered for the story as much as for the results: make sure it is your version of events which carries the day

the power web trap

Power management leads straight into a death trap: the cult of the hero leader. Business literature is full of great leaders who have turned round organisations by themselves. Newspapers are full of business heroes who make fortunes from their genius: they are also full of villains who made fortunes improperly or lost fortunes. The cult of the hero (or villain) businessperson is alive and well. Hero stories sell newspapers. Stories about complex systems send people to sleep.

Hero stories may be exciting, but they are also wrong.

The reality is that power does not lie with the individual: it lies in the power of the system. To check this reality, look at what happens to all the great leaders when they leave their power base. Most of them disappear into the irrelevance of committee and commission land where they can produce reports alongside other worthy but washed up ex-leaders. Warren Buffet, the legendary investor, has made a few billion dollars from understanding this and investing accordingly. Consider two of his maxims:

- "Only invest in a company which any fool can run, because some day some fool will run it."
- "When a manager with a great reputation joins an organisation with a lousy reputation, it is normally the reputation of the organisation which remains intact."

Buffet fully understands that power resides in the system, not in the individual. An effective leader will also understand this and use it to advantage. Instead of trying to do everything alone, the effective leader builds a team which can manage the whole system well. This requires pulling in diverse skills and the CEO has to pick a few battles where personal intervention will make a real difference. By doing less the CEO can achieve more.

Leadership is a team sport. Despite this, many leaders fall into the hero trap. They will have twenty or thirty years of experience telling them that they have a successful way of doing things. They do not take kindly to experts or colleagues suggesting that they may be wrong. And they have the power to make it not worthwhile for anyone to tell them that they are wrong. Given this, it is easy for senior people to believe that they alone can save the company or the nation. Look at how often leaders of nations stay on well beyond their sell-by date, in the naïve belief that they are somehow unique. Power is utterly addictive to anyone who tastes it: it should be a class A drug.

The result is that many people fall into the trap of thinking they need to be a hero: an implausible mix of Genghis Khan and Mother Theresa. Some managers think they are already that good: it is well worth not working for them. The desire for hero status is reinforced in large organisations where it can be difficult to stand out. The natural desire is to stake a claim to fame and to make it all your own, rather than sharing the glory.

Power is utterly addictive to anyone who tastes it

Effective managers do not try to do it all themselves. Effective managers make things happen through others. Behind every hero there is a team of good people who actually make things happen. No one does it all themselves. A good organisation will help ordinary people achieve extraordinary things. A poor organisation traps extraordinary people into achieving ordinary outcomes. Good or poor, organisations are complex beasts and a manager needs to harness all the capabilities of the beast to make things happen.

There are two main versions of the hero trap.

- The lone hero
- The guru in a box

The lone hero

The self-made millionaire entrepreneur falls into the classic hero trap. They follow the old saying, "If you want something done well, do it yourself." They often find it difficult to trust other people very far; they can be domineering and directive. They can also be very successful in their own right. If they are successful enough, they get a ghost-written autobiography which tells everyone that they should do it themselves as well.

The DIY (Do It Yourself) approach is more or less inevitable for entrepreneurs, at least when they start out. If you want to take the risks of starting up yourself, be prepared to go DIY. If you succeed, you will build a self-confidence bordering on arrogance and you will find it difficult to really respect and trust people who are content simply to be your wage slaves.

If you want to go DIY in a large organisation, you will fail.

The guru in a box

This is a very tempting trap for anyone who is good at their job, especially if it requires some form of specialist knowledge. The way for most people to progress early in their careers is to master their trade: sales, systems analysis, accounting or whatever functional skill you learn. Perform in your trade very well and you will probably be promoted. That is where the trouble starts.

Having discovered that expertise gets you promoted, some people seek to deepen their expertise even further. They do not realise that the rules of the game have changed. You are no longer the player on the pitch: you have become the team coach. You do not succeed as team coach by trying to play harder and better than ever before. You have to coach the team and help them achieve the best performance possible, rather than trying to play yourself.

Within an organisation, the guru in a box is easy to spot. They are the people who take on all the hardest technical challenges. This makes them a great resource to the organisation, but in terms of power they are heading into the wilderness. They are not building their team, because they are keeping all the tough challenges for themselves rather than delegating them and coaching the team to overcome the challenges. They are not building the networks of power which will enable them to progress. After a few years they realise they are going nowhere and either get very frustrated, or commit themselves to a career as an expert.

Strong PQ managers learn that the rules of the game change as your career progresses. Moving from being a great player to being a great coach is the first big step on the road to PQ success.

The guru in a box trap

David was very smart. That was the problem which was holding him back: he was trapped in the prison of success.

When he first joined the organisation he was given the one task no one else wanted: he was asked to create a business case to justify a $100 million systems project for a UK life insurance company. The client had already spent $70 million, and was starting to ask if it was going to see any return on its investment. This was a question which the technology consultants had desperately been hoping to avoid.

David did a stellar job, much to everyone's surprise. In career terms, it was a disaster for David. Suddenly he got drawn into doing business cases for every systems project for every UK life insurer. He was the classic "expert in a box". He would be brought into a project, let out of his box to work his magic and then firmly put back in the box once he had performed his magic trick on the numbers.

There is, possibly, a career to be carved out of the arcane world of business cases for systems projects for UK life insurers. It is not a career with great prospects, and it is not a career which David wanted. Three years later, he was still trying to escape the assignment treadmill which made him repeat the same trick time and again.

It pays to be not too good at things you do not want to do.

how: earning the currency of power

Earning the currency of power is a mixture of substance and style. Power has several currencies, some of which are stronger than others. You need to recognise and earn the real thing, not the fake. The three main currencies of power are:

- Fear
- Love
- Trust

The strongest currency, and the hardest to earn, is trust.

High PQ managers not only earn the currency of power, they show they have it. They do not hide all their currency in a bank vault: they make sure people see they have power. Style counts. If you appear powerful, people will treat you as if you are powerful. If you appear weak, people will treat you as if you are weak. Style counts. The style guide to power is based on three pillars:

- The appearance of power
- The language of power
- The behaviour of power: the partnership principle

the currency of power

Traditionally, there have been two ways of exercising power: by being feared or being liked.

The power of fear

Machiavelli wrote 500 years ago in *The Prince* that "it is better to be feared than loved". This was sound advice for a hierarchical world. Love is fickle, but fear can be managed and controlled. In a command and control workplace there is still little choice about who you work with. You are assigned a team and a boss and that is who you work with. It is not necessary to want to work with the team and the boss: you have to work with them. There are still plenty of bosses out there who work on the fear principle. It works, but only in a limited way. Fear earns compliance, not commitment: staff do what they have to, no more. Fear does not bring out the best in people in the long term. And it has little effect on people over whom the boss has no control: the boss just looks like a petty tyrant to people outside his or her sphere of control.

In complicated organisations, we need the support of a wide range of people over whom we can not exercise control and in whom we can instil little fear. We can not compel them to give us the priority and focus we think we merit. We have to gain their commitment. Fear does not build commitment.

The power of love

Many leaders want to be liked and think that being liked is essential to success. They are wrong. You do not need to be liked to be effective.

Once again, the cause of this misunderstanding is the leadership literature which extols the virtue of the charismatic and inspirational leader. Leaders are urged to be charismatic and inspirational so that they can create devoted followers who will love, honour and obey them. If you have charisma and inspiration, you are lucky. They are not learnable skills and the charisma transplant has not yet been devised by the medical profession. Charisma and inspiration are powerful, but dangerous characteristics. For every charismatic leader who leads you to the Promised Land, there are a dozen who lead you straight back into the desert. Charisma does not make a leader infallible, honest or moral. The charismatic leader also tends to fall into the hero trap outlined in the last section: they make themselves look good at the expense of creating a sustainable organisation.

You do not need to be liked to be effective

The charisma myth is supported by leadership surveys that show that we want charismatic and inspirational leaders, and that we do not have them. This proves that there is a charisma gap. It also proves that such surveys are rubbish. If you ask people if they want a million dollars, most people will say yes. Ask them if they have a million dollars, and most will say they do not. This indicates a widespread million dollar gap. Wanting something is not the same as needing something. We may like charismatic leaders (although Hitler, Mao Tse Tung, Pol Pot and most murdering dictators were charismatic at some point in their careers), but they are not always good.

For every charismatic leader who leads you to the Promised Land, there are a dozen who lead you straight back into the desert

We do not need to be charismatic to succeed. Look around your own organisation. There are probably not too many executives you would accuse of being charismatic. Despite this, there are probably quite a few executives that are highly effective and make things happen. They are probably the better role models for PQ and for making things happen than the charismatic Hitler or Pol Pot.

Being liked and being feared are dead ends on the road to effectiveness. We need to find an alternative, PQ path to making things happen.

The power of trust

Most leaders lack the power to rely on fear or the charisma to rely on love. Leaders do not need to rely on fear or love. Leaders can be devastatingly effective by building networks based on trust. Look at it from the other perspective: do you want to work with or for someone whom you do not trust? You may have to work with such a person occasionally, but you are likely to avoid doing so as much as possible. In a world where formal hierarchies and control mechanisms are breaking down, trust is the currency of power and influence.

Trust does not emerge randomly. There is a way that we either earn or lose trust: we can all remember moments when someone has earned or lost trust with us. There is a simple formula for thinking about how you build trust. Here it is in all its spurious mathematical accuracy:

$$T = (V \times C)/R$$

T = Trust. This is the currency you are attempting to earn with each member of your power network.

V = Values intimacy. Put simply: do you share common interests, values, experiences and aspirations? If you do, you are likely to find yourself getting on well. If you do not, then start working hard to find some point of common interest: it can be places you have lived or worked, people you know in common, any point of commonality gives you a starting point.

C = Credibility. You might find you have much in common with someone, and you may enjoy going out for a drink with them. That does not mean you trust them. There needs to be credibility as well: they need to be able to deliver on what they say. If they are all talk and no walk, then there is no trust.

R = Risk. Risk is the largely submerged, unseen iceberg which sinks relationships and sinks decisions. It is also the reason that trust builds incrementally. You have to demonstrate credibility on small things first, and then slowly build up to larger things.

building trust to gain power

Building trust takes time. The more you know someone, the easier it is to tune into their likes and dislikes; the longer you have worked with someone, the more of a track record you have built up which demonstrates your credibility. This poses the challenge of how to build trust when you are new to an organisation or you are meeting new people. You start off with essentially zero trust, and yet you need to acquire it fast if people are going to work with you.

Building values intimacy

Building values intimacy can give you a quick start in the first meeting: show you have similar interests, values, experiences and aspirations. The first and easiest step is the desk challenge. As you go into someone's office, note what is on their walls or desk. There are normally many giveaways:

- Picture of vintage car, home, exotic holiday destination, skiing, sports team: they are advertising their personal interests. Ask about them, especially if you can link yourself to any of them
- Picture of family: advertising their family. Useful, especially if you have family at the same stage
- Diplomas are a sign of someone with professional pride, or vanity: let them talk

If you are in a meeting room, all the visual clues will be absent. But if you have done your homework you should know something about them already. You should be able to find that you have some point of common experience (organisations you have both encountered) or have people whom you both know. The chances are that you have been introduced by someone you both have in common. Find the common starting point, and let them talk.

At this early stage, many people try to make an impression by boasting about their great experience. This is a mistake. It simply invites critical questions and does nothing to build a relationship. This is where you need to discover the essential secret of all good leaders and power brokers: they have two ears and one mouth. This probably means you have the secret of leadership and power. Next, learn how to use these secret weapons. The rule is simple: use them in the proportion stated. Listen twice as much (two ears) as you speak (one mouth).

Let people talk about their favourite subject: themselves. You will find that clients have an unnerving habit of talking themselves into sales, managers talk themselves into agreement and lovers talk themselves into bed. Whether you want to talk your clients or managers into bed is your decision. As they talk, they will give you plenty of clues for you to follow up on. As you listen, they will convince themselves that you must be very smart to share the same great perspective on the world as they have. You do not need to put forward any arguments. Simply empathise with what they say and ask a few open questions to keep them talking.

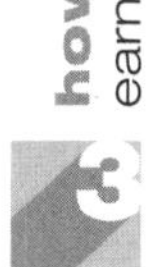

You do not need to flatter people: let them flatter themselves. We all have a self image which we are likely to express if we are given the chance. Typical self images include people who think they are:

- Insightful
- Generous
- Kind to others
- Technically brilliant
- Adventurous
- Loyal
- Brave in the face of overwhelming odds
- Important and successful

Normally, they will not say, "I am brave, insightful and generous." But they will tell you stories in which they demonstrate their preferred self image. When you show great interest and admiration for this story, they will be happy to know that they have found a soul mate or supporter for their world view.

Winning friends

Vanessa was professionally late. It was a sort of personal policy decision of hers to arrive to anything, even a breakfast meeting, at least fifteen minutes late. Perhaps it was a power play: it was her way of saying, "I am so busy I can not turn up on time, and I am so important I can keep you waiting." It was not a great way of making yourself liked.

We were both due to meet a very important prospective client at 11am. I turned up and started the meeting at 11am. It was a tough meeting with lots of issues coming up, but I thought we were making progress. At around 11.20am she made a dramatic entrance, flashing smiles and apologies at everyone. She flirted with the men, not realising that the senior client was a woman and was getting really irritated by the flirting.

She then changed the agenda away from the substance of the meeting to talking about people and who knew who and what they were doing. My jaw dropped. She was gossiping. Again. She was always gossiping in meetings. I thought she was an old windbag; she thought I had the interpersonal skills of a pterodactyl on a bad day. We did not realise it at the time, but we were the perfect team.

After fifteen minutes of gossip (fifteen minutes which I thought we could not afford) she had established who knew who, and in the process had established her credibility. They all swapped stories about what was going on and, despite her late entrance and her airs and graces, they were all getting on very well with each other. It was like an old friends' reunion party. I began to feel like a gatecrasher at the party.

After the gossip, Vanessa steered the conversation to a gentle chat about the client's business. She let the client talk about their challenges, and boast about their achievements. Another fifteen precious minutes passed. But even I noticed their behaviour change. They started to relax. Their guard came down. They began to like us, or at least Vanessa; they saw her as on their side. They were talking themselves into agreement with us.

In the end we did not even need to sell to them. With ten minutes to go, the senior client looked at her watch and said, "Time is nearly up. I know you need to talk about this proposal. I am sure it can help us. I have to go, but I would be delighted if you can work out the details with the team."

to win an argument, first win a friend

The meeting had gone from being tough to being a walkover. I had learned that to win an argument, first win a friend. I was building the logical case, Vanessa was building the relationship. That is why we made the perfect team: one of us worked logic, the other worked emotion. I wondered how much more we could achieve if she could turn up on time...

Building credibility

The next step is to move from building values intimacy to building credibility. This is where you have to start performing. The fundamental tenet of building credibility is that of the perfect postman: you always deliver. The inscription on the James Farley Post Office in New York sums it up:

> "Neither snow nor rain nor heat nor gloom of night stays these couriers from the swift completion of their appointed rounds."

That inscription is based on a passage from Herodotus, the Roman historian, talking about the courier service in ancient Persia. The credibility that comes from delivery is eternal. Excuses are the rust in trust: they are utterly corrosive of the credibility you are trying to build. Like the great courier, you need to overcome obstacles, not use them as excuses for failing to deliver.

Building credibility takes time. In the short term you can borrow some credibility, which at least gives you the chance to earn some credibility in your own right. Borrowed credibility is essentially an endorsement from a trusted third party. Sources of borrowed credibility include:

- A strong brand name employer (you never get fired for hiring IBM, or McKinsey: even if they mess up, you can not be faulted for hiring the best)
- References from a previous employer or from satisfied clients
- Professional qualifications: endorsement from a recognised body
- Introduction by a trusted intermediary
- Instructions you are following from a big boss in your organisation

Borrowed credibility does little more than buy you time. You can not sustain a career by always arguing for your position by saying, "But that is what the boss wants..." You need to establish your own credibility.

There are a few things you can do immediately to make a mark:

- Always return phone calls and emails promptly
- Write up and circulate meeting notes within hours, not days: they will be easier to write when fresh, saves time later and looks highly professional
- Brief people well before meetings to set clear expectations about roles, outcomes and logistics: avoid any surprises
- Add value: if you know someone has an interest in a topic, make sure you let them see any relevant articles, data or information which may help them
- Conspicuous honesty: always return a borrowed pen, dropped small change or lost notes to their rightful owner. The biggest crooks and fraudsters learn that if you are honest on the small things, you can misuse your talents on the large things

Being positive and looking the part: this is covered in more detail in section 3.

Equally, there are plenty of things you can do to mess up. Some classic examples:

- Bad numbers in a presentation: one bad number undermines every other number and the presenter
- Spelling errors: if you can not spell, do not expect anyone to trust your arguments either
- Gossiping and bad mouthing people behind their backs, which prompts this natural reaction: "If you say that about them when their backs are turned, what do you say about me when my back is turned?"
- Excuses and blaming other people when things go wrong. Don't look back: look forward to what you will do to remedy the situation
- Over claiming and boasting about successes: do not try to hog all the limelight No one will believe you did it all yourself, and they will not want to work with someone who will steal all the credit for their efforts. Be generous

From these small starts, you build credibility and power one step at a time. Each time you achieve one goal, you earn the right to take on a slightly more challenging goal.

Managing risk

Risk is the unseen and unspoken fear that undermines progress, kills decisions and destroys power. Managed well, risk can also be a short cut to power.

Most people dislike risk. This has nothing to do with the risk logs much beloved of consultants and of non-executive directors who want to prove their worth. That is rational risk which most managers and organisations can handle. Dangerous risk is personal and political. It normally comes in the form of unspoken questions such as:

- If this change goes ahead, how will it affect me?
- If this project goes wrong, what happens to me?
- If I get the new boss, what does it mean for my prospects?

- If I take on this assignment, does that help me or hinder me?
- Am I better off opposing or supporting this new initiative?
- What's in it for me: my career, my workload, my bonus and promotion prospects?

These are questions that managers ask themselves all the time. But they are not seen as legitimate questions in public. The result is that the most important questions (personal and political questions) get hidden behind a smokescreen of rational debate. Instead of arguing against a new idea because it will cause someone too much extra work, they will find endless rational arguments against it. This becomes a very dysfunctional exercise. The rational debate gets more and more intense with both sides digging in harder than ever because they are trying to protect personal and political positions.

The high PQ manager recognises that management is not purely rational. It is intensely personal (emotional) and political as well. Manage the politics and the rational arguments will manage themselves.

When "no" means "yes"

We thought we had worked the politics very well. We had lined up various government ministers in support of the new idea. We had lined up the critical delivery agency to support the new idea. All we now needed was for the civil servants to go through the normal procedures and we would be able to start the new programme.

We went to the final meeting, all ready to get started. Then the civil servants dropped a bombshell. They said "no". They gave us very clear reasons why the programme should not go ahead. They said it was far too risky and was likely to fail.

We left the meeting dispirited: months of work had gone down the drain. We thought more closely about what they said. We knew that it was nonsense to say the programme was risky and might fail: we were convinced it was bound to succeed. And then we realised that the risk to the civil servants was not failure: it was success. If our programme succeeded, it would make their programmes look ineffective and expensive by comparison. Our success would embarrass them and their ministers.

So we decided to go back to the civil servants in private. We paid lip service to the rational risk of failure. If we had argued that it was going to be a big success, we would have fuelled all their worst nightmares. They would have opposed us 100%. Instead, we spent most of the time convincing them that this would be a very modest and discreet success which would not embarrass them at all.

At the next formal meeting with the civil servants and ministers, we got approval. In the end, our programme was a big success which forced them to close down their competing programmes. Having won the war, we made sure we won the peace as well by giving the ministers and civil servants all the credit for backing our idea.

Four simple principles help managers manage risk to their advantage:

1 When someone makes a rational statement for or against an idea, immediately ask, "Why are they taking that position?" Understand the politics behind the logic

2 Manage political risk in private, not in public. Once someone has taken a position in public, it becomes very difficult for them politically to change that position. Any meeting with more than two people present is a public meeting. In private, find out what their agenda is

3 If in doubt, remove the risk. Most normal people (this excludes entrepreneurs, consultants, CEOs and investment bankers) hate risk and uncertainty because they can not control it and they may lose from it. If you are the person who can remove the risk, ambiguity and uncertainty, you are likely to gain allies fast

4 Manage risk incrementally. As you build trust and confidence, the incremental approach is essential. Build your own credibility fast and early by delivering on small things (meeting minutes done well and fast, for instance). Test others

on small things first. See if they can deliver on simple tasks and promises to start with. As confidence builds on both sides, you can progress to bigger and more challenging tasks

creating the appearance of power: pace, space and grace

Some people ooze charisma and power. Other people ooze failure. And some people ooze slime. These would seem to be inherited characteristics: you have it, or you don't. While there are some people who are clearly beyond the reach of any power makeover, there are many small things you can do to increase your appearance of power. The simplest principle to remember is the motto of Sir William Lyons, the founder of Jaguar. He insisted that the hallmark of all Jaguars should be "pace, space and grace". The hallmark of an effective power manager is also pace, space and grace.

Power shopping: the tale of two high streets

Brick Lane, in East London, is a poor neighbourhood sitting in the shadow of the most extraordinary wealth in the City, the financial services district of London. Going there from the City is a distance of about 400 metres physically and about 4,000 kilometres economically. In place of all the sophisticated financial markets there are market stalls and shops piled high with bargains: fruit and vegetables which had been rejected by the supermarket chains; endless cheap plastic ware, bargain fabrics and end of line or surplus goods from manufacturers. In the vast mountains of stuff, you know you should be able to find a real bargain or two.

If, instead of heading east to Brick Lane, you head west to Bond Street you will find a completely different shopping experience. There are jewellery shops and fashion shops each with one or two exquisite items tastefully displayed in the front window. Naturally, no prices are displayed. If you have to ask, you probably should not be in the shop anyway. If you pluck up the courage to go into a fashion shop, you will find relatively little stock on the shop floor. A few items will be displayed carefully while unctuous assistants ask sir or madam if they can be of any assistance.

Retailers understand the psychology well. Pile it high and sell it cheap in Brick Lane. Keep it very exclusive, expensive and discreet in Bond Street: less (stock) is more (price and exclusivity).

Power managers use the same principle. While salespeople and juniors go through their patter and say more and more to make their case, the power players understand that saying less has more effect. By saying less, they listen more and learn more which enables them to make a better intervention. By saying one or two things very clearly, they make more impact than the junior who says lots of things. One clear message is far more powerful than many conflicting messages.

One clear message is far more powerful than many conflicting messages

Pace and power

Pace is about how much you say and when you say it.

Aristocrats used to say that "new money shouts, old money whispers". This was their way of saying that they had class, but not much money, while rich tradesmen might have money but they had no class. From this simple insight generations of aristocrats sought to intermarry with rich businesspeople to get their money, while the businesspeople wanted to buy into some class.

As with money, so with power. New power shouts, old power whispers. Look at how meetings go when there are several levels of seniority present. Very junior people may say nothing and probably should not be there: no power is mute. The emerging power brokers will all be trying to make an impact, make their pitch and present their case. They will be making high effort. Meanwhile the most senior person may say very little other than to ask some questions, run the agenda and draw out the decisions and conclusions.

In practice, this is a hierarchy which is hard to avoid in public meetings. Senior people have the power and privilege of saying less, while the junior people have to work hard to make their point and their voice heard. The solution is to avoid having decisions made in public meetings. There are three problems with decision making in a public meeting:

- The decision may be the wrong decision
- Once a decision is made in public, it is very hard to reverse
- You are not in control: it is at best a fair contest. You do not want a fair contest: you want a done deal

The solution is to work as much of an agenda as possible in private, one to one. Square off each constituency in private. Listen to their concerns, deal with them privately. Only use the public meeting to give public confirmation to the private consensus you have built.

Once in power, the less you say the more impact each word has. If you are always sounding off, people will quickly learn to ignore most of what you say. If you say little, you force them to take notice and there is less opportunity for mixed messages to come out.

Pace is not just about how much you say. It is also about when you say it. An old adage in rugby football is "get your retaliation in first": hit the opponent before they hit you. The same goes for negotiating a position. The essential principle is to anchor the discussion early around your needs, before someone else anchors the discussion around their needs. The classic example of this is budget discussions. If you wait until the first draft budget comes out of the planning department, you are likely to be dead meat. You will be arguing the fine details of what the finance group think you can achieve, which is unlikely to be what you think you can achieve to get a great bonus. You need to pre-empt the whole discussion.

If you wait until the first draft budget comes out of the planning department, you are likely to be dead meat

For instance, when I was running a business in Japan I bumped into our CEO (deliberately) over coffee at a conference.

> "How's Japan now?" asked the CEO.
>
> "Better. We can hit break even next year, if we can get the new IT system and the two expats we talked about earlier in the year."
>
> "No more red ink?" asked the surprised CEO.
>
> "Not if we get the investment", I replied, with fingers firmly crossed.

That year's budget discussion was anchored entirely around a discussion about how much investment and how close to break even we could reasonably get. If the finance director had got to the CEO first, the discussion would have been about a minimum 10% margin and no investment. Say goodbye to your bonus and hello to hard work for the next year.

Most budget and planning discussions rapidly get bogged down in fine tuning the detail. This absorbs a huge amount of time and political effort. If you anchor the discussion early enough around your assumptions, then you can relax about the fine tuning and can gain political goodwill by conceding on some of the detail.

Space and power

The importance of space is obvious to anyone who has walked out of cubicle land and into the C-suite. The carpets are thicker, the flowers are fresher and the newspapers are today's; the cacophony and chaos of the cubicle is replaced by the hush and plush of power. Whatever physical space you have, there are two things you can do to use space to convey power: clean your space and personalise your space.

I was long ago told that a tidy desk is the sign of a tidy mind. The manager who told me that had a wooden desk which appeared to be empty: I wondered what sort of a mind that was a sign of. I have struggled ever since to keep a tidy desk: not because it shows a tidy mind, but because it is a sign of power. The hallmark of a junior manager is a desk piled high with papers and other stuff. Some people think this shows that they are working very hard. To others it shows that they are disorganised, not in control and do not have a secretary. Although I have worked with one CEO whose desk was like a war zone and who carried papers in large plastic shopping bags, he was the exception. He was also fired. Most CEOs have pretty calm spaces. Ditch the dirty cups, old sandwich boxes and funny souvenirs from abroad; put as much paper as you can in the Number One File (the trash can) and file the rest. As with much of power, less is more.

People like to personalise their office space: it is a way of marking out our territory. Posters of your favourite sports team or movie star, or of your family and holiday snaps may seem harmless, but they are at best useless. It says something about you, but it says nothing about your power, performance or prospects. Personalise your space to your advantage: use it to promote yourself. Pictures of you doing something genuinely interesting, difficult or impressive say more about your power than pictures of a three year old. This does not mean you need to use Photoshop® to doctor images so that presidents and monarchs appear to be hanging onto your every word. It can be as simple as pictures of you giving out awards for some charity where you are a trustee; instead of the motivational poster of someone else climbing an impossible mountain, perhaps it is a picture of you climbing an impossible mountain. You simply need to convey the image that you are a fundamentally successful and interesting person outside work as well as at work.

Grace and power

Dress for success sounds very shallow, and it is. People should not be judged by how they look, but they are. It pays to look the part. If you dress in street smart loserwear, slouch like a teenager in full hormonal angst, think hygiene is for wimps and have enough pins and studs in your face to cause panic at airport security, do not expect an immediate invitation to join the board. Instead, you need to read the real dress code of your organisation. This code is likely to be as finely tuned as uniforms in the military, with different uniforms for different ranks, services and activities. If in doubt, dress like a good role model one level above you, who may or may not be your boss. Dress codes now vary dramatically, not just by country but also by:

- Industry: creative types in the media dress differently from conservative types in banks and central government
- Function: engineering staff versus marketing staff
- Level: board room versus the post room
- Activity: meeting clients may require suits, attending a training event may require informal dress

Inevitably, this leads to massive confusion. Large IT firms want to be seen as cool and funky high tech in the graduate recruiting market place, and yet be sober and reliable partners of global clients in the customer market place. They get to wear lots of different uniforms.

The dress caste system is very clear when flying. Suits and ties are largely absent in the cheap seats; business class is the land of the suit; first class reverts to expensive casual. The best sign of power is when you no longer have to wear the uniform of the road warrior: you have graduated from road warrior to master of the universe and can play to your own rules.

Dress for success does not always mean dressing up. It often means dressing discreetly. In days gone by the king used to be the most extravagantly dressed person, and no one dared to outdress the king. Now roles are reversed. Real power is discreet. Look at pictures of meetings of the G8 countries: the most powerful people on the planet are dressed in unobtrusive suits, while the ceremonial guards who have zero power are dressed as flamboyantly as the kings of days gone by.

Grace is not just about dress: it is about behaviour. It is hard to be graceful in the time pressured and resource constrained ranks of middle management. It may be hard, but try it. One of the sim-

Power dressing

I was very pleased with myself. The interview had gone so well that the interviewer had offered me a placement on the spot. As I was leaving the room he stopped me. "There's just one thing", he said, looking at my grease-stained boiler suit and safety boots which I had been working in, "We work in an office. You will need to buy a suit before you start."

Some years later, I was once again pleased with myself as the partner offered me a job in his firm. He then coughed quietly and looked at my rather old and shabby suit. "One of the advantages of joining the firm is that we can advance you the first month's salary. So if you need to buy a new suit, or some decent shoes…" his voice trailed off.

Some years later the senior partner was delighted to admit me to the partnership. "I must introduce you to some of the other partners", he said, "but before I do that, let me introduce you to my personal tailor…"

Not all of us are naturally graceful; nor do we necessarily care about it. Unfortunately, even if you don't care other people care about it greatly. To act the part, they expect you to look the part. Like any actor, you need not just a script: you need the right costume as well. Then you can be the star of the show.

plest tactics is to thank people and praise people in public. This has two main benefits:

- It is an easy way to win friends
- It puts you in a position of power

Praising people may seem an odd way of showing power. It could also be seen to be risky: if I praise someone for the work they have done, will they get all the credit instead of me? In fact, the reverse is true. By doling out the praise you are making the statement that you are the one who was really in control, really knew who was doing what. You are not giving away the credit for a job well done: you are taking the credit without having to fight anyone for it.

Sharing the limelight

Francis was brighter than the midday sun. This was unnerving for the rest of us who struggled to shine much more brightly than a 40 watt bulb. He would always be at least three steps ahead of us, but he was smart enough not to upset us by demonstrating his intellectual superiority over us.

In meetings, he was very self-effacing. He would stay quiet and listen to our nonsense. He would only step in when we had exhausted and confused ourselves. Then he would carefully summarise: he would pick up on some point that each person had made and say what a wonderful, creative and original point it was. You would watch each person round the table starting to puff themselves up with pride to be praised that way. They also started to realise that Francis must be a wonderful and insightful ally to be so supportive of their comments. By the end of his summary, everyone would be on his side and ready to endorse more or less any idea he was carefully positioning. Naturally, the ideas were all his: he was simply making sure that we thought they were our own so that we would support him.

He never tried to take the credit, but he always got his way. He also built a formidable set of allies right across the organisation.

Someone who was slightly less smart would have used their intellectual muscle to beat us into submission. Francis was not just intellectually smart (IQ). He was also politically smart (PQ): he was smart enough to make us think that his ideas were our ideas. No one argues against their own ideas.

the language of power

Mind your language. How you say things counts. As you listen to people talk, you will find they normally fall into one of three modes:

- Hype
- Positive
- Negative

The language of power is positive. A quick tour through each mode shows why.

Hype

We live in an age of hype. C-list celebrities are billed as supernova megastars and newspapers translate minor setbacks or advances into disasters and breakthroughs. Hype has seeped into the language of business. Everything is now strategic: strategic is used to describe everything from acquiring your major competitor through to redesigning the floor plan of head office. Hype is essentially about misusing and overusing power words. Every business and industry has its own favourite hype words. Typical examples of power words which are routinely misused include:

> strategic, important, transformation, breakthrough, urgent, mission critical, radical, paradigm, world class, excellence.

Speakers often like to ally hype words to the latest management trend such as:

> six sigma, reengineering, core competencies, strategic intent, value innovation and co-creation.

Entire presentations can be built by mixing power words and trend words into a parody of management speak. Hype often impresses the speaker, but rarely impresses the alert listener. By overselling everything, the hypester quickly loses credibility and devalues the message. When they speak about something which is truly strategic, no one believes them: they sound just the same as when they spoke about the strategic redeployment of the coffee machines.

Power words need to be used sparingly and with impact. If you avoid calling everything urgent and important, then the day you declare something is important and urgent, people will take notice and they will be inclined to believe you.

Positive language

Positive language projects confidence and certainty. These are valuable commodities in organisations where ambiguity and uncertainty are commonplace. A few examples will make the point.

- "We will…" versus "We might…". "Will" is positive. "Might" and other conditionals such as "could" or "may" convey uncertainty and doubt. Power is not built by being uncertain. You need to have, and to project, confidence
- "We need to gain the support of…" versus "If we have the support of…". "If" not only conveys uncertainty, it also carries the seeds of failure together with the ready made excuse for why we failed. "We need to…" drives to action and takes responsibility for achieving the outcome. "We need to…" is a neat way of framing challenges and problems in a positive way
- "We found that…" versus "Under further in-depth analysis it has been ascertained that…" Positive language is short, clear and crisp. It avoids the passive ("it has been…"). Speaking and writing simply aids understanding

Inevitably, it is possible to be too positive and to make rash promises when saying, "We will…" Do not leave hostages to fortune. "We will…" can simply refer to some simple next steps rather than delivering some amazing outcome in the future.

Negative language

Being negative is a good way of avoiding taking responsibility. It is also a good way of avoiding power: no responsibility means no power.

Spare a thought for your colleagues. They have enough problems of their own without you adding to them by being negative or just passive. They want help and solutions: if you are negative you become an energy sink for the rest of the organisation. The language to watch for here includes both straightforward negative comments and, more dangerously, questions. Questions often appear helpful and insightful. In practice, they are often used to create uncertainty, doubt, conflict and more work. Typical negative language includes:

- We can't...
- Not possible...
- Are you sure...
- Have you thought of...
- Risky...

Pride of place in the pantheon of negative language goes to "But" as in:

- I agree but...
- You did really well but...
- That might work but...

Remember that everything before "but" is meadow mayonnaise. Ignore what was said before "but" because they do not mean it: focus only on what they said after the "but".

behaving powerfully: the partnership principle

If you act like a junior person, you will be treated like a junior person. If you act like a serious player, you have a chance of being treated seriously.

In many organisations bosses and staff get stuck in a parent–child script. Good parent bosses may help, support and nurture their charges. Bad parent bosses just shout at, direct and abuse their charges. Either way, the power relationship is all one way. Some of this is unavoidable. At bonus and promotion time, the hierarchy will reassert itself in even the most democratic organisation.

If you act like a junior person, you will be treated like a junior person

You do not have to be stuck with the parent–child script all the time. If you want to build and project power, you need to build an adult to adult script: you need to build a partnership with senior executives. Once they treat you as an equal, they are likely to make you an equal. Being treated as an equal involves some basic behaviour changes.

Focus on their agenda, not yours. Understand where the power brokers are coming from and what their agenda looks like. Then shape your agenda around theirs. When you do this, you move from pleading and pitching your case, to working with them to help them move forward their agenda. You become their partner, not their subordinate. Understanding their agenda takes time and you will need your network of coaches and mentors to advise you.

Ditch PowerPoint. Now. PowerPoint presentations put you in the role of the defendant pleading a case while the bosses sit back and judge you. They are not on your side: they are assessing you. Instead of the big public PowerPoint presentation, discuss your idea in private with the key power brokers. Seek their advice as much as their support: if they advise you, they are likely to support you anyway. You gently move them from being your judge to your partner. That is a far more powerful position to occupy.

If you must resort to PowerPoint, keep it short. Apply the 10–20–30 rule: no more than ten pages, minimum twenty point typeface and maximum thirty minutes presentation. Large typeface stops you putting too many words on the page. Brevity forces you to focus on what is important: you may have plenty of detail in your back pocket, but keep it there. Junior people get lost in detail. Boring your bosses is not a good way to persuade them.

Keep memos short. As with PowerPoint, brevity helps focus on the right issues. P&G was the land of the one page memo: young brand assistants had to summarise two months of brand business onto one page. If the progress of a business, with indicated actions going forward, can be summarised on one page, then most other things can be summarised on one page as well.

Act the part. Goofing around and bad mouthing management is great for cynical and junior managers who wish to stay that way: cynical and junior.

How to ask for a billion dollars

I decided to start my own bank. This is a rather expensive exercise. A quick calculation showed that I would need about a billion dollars to fund the operations and to provide the capital to keep the regulators happy. I checked my bank account: I was at least $999 million dollars short of my goal. As an unemployed person on the street, it was not immediately obvious who was going to cough up that much money for me. I could not see my local bank manager helping me start a rival to put him out of a job.

I used my networks to set up meetings with various banks. Eventually, substantive talks started with one of them. I had several meetings with the CEO and eventually we got to the crunch meeting: I knew it was important because it was just the two of us sitting but not relaxing on the sofas in his office. Eventually, he asked the key question:

> *"How much?"*
>
> *"About a billion", I replied, as casually as possible "Over five years, most of it is success capital, regulatory capital."*
>
> *"Dollars or pounds?" he asked without raising an eyelid.*
>
> *"Pounds", I said, deciding to give myself another few hundred million dollars of room to manoeuvre.*
>
> *"Good", he said. "If you had asked for any less, you would not have been serious."*

I then realised that until that point I had put virtually no paper in front of him in any meeting. No PowerPoint presentations, no Excel® spreadsheets and no long memos. We had simply been talking the idea through in some detail. If I had come in with PowerPoint presentations, I would have been just like all his subordinates coming in and making their pitch. Instead, I had positioned myself as his partner and equal, and got treated that way.

After the agreement in principle, we produced the detailed plans. I then discovered that business plans attract no IP (Intellectual Property) rights in the UK. They got a great bank and I got some great experience.

The partnership principle describes effective behaviour across hierarchies. It also describes effective behaviour in negotiations. Inspirational speakers who urge you to "negotiate to win!" and "close that sale!" and "use an exclamation mark!" are dangerous. They live in the world of win/lose negotiations. Making your negotiating partner into a loser is fine if you never need to see them, meet them or negotiate with them again: then you can stiff them as much as you want. In reality, most of the time you will be negotiating with partners who you will have to deal with on a regular basis. You need to treat them as partners and find a win/win solution, not a win/lose one.

Achieving the win/win is not easy. It means moving beyond superficial positions (get the best price) to understanding interests. Perhaps the buyer wants a low price on a component, but the buyer's real interest may be in the lowest lifetime cost of the complete product: if your component reduces total lifetime costs, then perhaps they will be prepared to pay more for it, not less. To understand a buyer's interest (low lifetime costs) versus position (low component price today) requires changing from salesperson mindset to partner mindset. Instead of pushing a product, you need to listen and understand what the buyer really needs: you have to work with them, not against them.

Ultimately, the partnership principle encourages cooperation, not competition. Cooperation is the PQ way of winning without fighting.

when:
seize the moment

We have all seen moments where power ebbs or flows away from someone. Years of hard work can disappear in a moment of madness. Gerald Ratner, an entrepreneur, built up a large chain of successful jewellery shops. He was in great demand on the speaking circuit as an example of successful enterprise. In one speech he made a joke where he compared some cheap trinkets in his shops unfavourably with a prawn sandwich. The media latched onto this joke. Immediately, the credibility and quality of his jewellery chain was wrecked: the chain was shortly taken over and renamed. Years of work destroyed because of a misjudged joke.

Equally, a crisis can be the making of a leader. Rudolph Giuliani cemented his leadership credentials with the way he handled the 9/11 crisis as Mayor of New York: it was a performance which drew great credit compared to the faltering performance of the President.

Many moments of truth can not be predicted, but they can be planned for. The essence of seizing the moment is taking control. With planned events, you can plan to take control. With unplanned events, there is a moment when everyone is uncertain what to do and how to do it: most people wait to see what the safe course of action will be. That is the safe PQ response to uncertainty. The high PQ response is to be the person who takes control and defines the safe course of action for everyone else to follow.

The critical events which managers need to prepare for include:

- Meetings
- Presentations
- Persuading and influencing people
- Overcoming resistance
- Stopping bad ideas
- Managing crises
- Dealing with awkward people

Behind all of these events lies one key principle: strike early and take control. The later you leave things, the worse they are likely to become and the less control you are likely to have. Before exploring each of the moments of truth, we will look at why striking early is so important.

striking early and seizing control

In any organisation there are critical moments marked by uncertainty, risk and ambiguity. No one is quite sure what to do. Most people sit on the sidelines and wait until they see what the safest course of action will be. Joining the herd is always safe: even if you are wrong, you are no more wrong than everyone else. Survival means following the herd; success means leading it. A high PQ manager will learn to take calculated risks and to strike early, when the ambiguity risk and opportunity is still high. By the time the ambiguity has gone, so has most of the opportunity. Typical moments of ambiguity which can be exploited are:

Survival means following the herd; success means leading it

- Will this new product/initiative/idea work and who will staff it?
- How do we respond to this crisis?
- Who will sort out the mess in function/department/business X?
- What will our annual offsite meeting look like and who will take the lead?

The critical moment is often fleeting and informal: it may consist of a short discussion round a table. The first person to blink is the one who volunteers. The volunteer has become the leader who will come up with the plan. Within a week or two, many other people will be jostling for position and arguing who should be on or off the team. By striking very early, you assume the most powerful position without the need for political in-fighting: you have pre-empted all the key battles.

These moment can not always be predicted, although your network should be giving you early warning of such opportunities. But you can always be prepared for such opportunities. Preparation means having a positive mindset which is always asking, "How can I make the most of this situation?" instead of "How can I avoid more work, risks and problems as a result of this situation?"

Striking early and taking control: three stories

An uncharitable act
The charity was just starting up. A kindly businessperson volunteered to do all the grubby administrative work of dealing with the Charity Commission and lawyers. We let him take control of that part of the agenda. He used this to appoint himself as chairman and his friends as trustees. Five years later, he and his cronies were still installed as the chairman and trustees, without adding any notable value to the charity at all. If you control the right part of the agenda, you control everything.

Exploiting skeletons
The business unit was in some distress. The management team was putting in a huge amount of effort to sort out existing contracts, get current projects back on track and to build a stable backlog of clients and business. A member of the Head Office Finance Department volunteered to go and help by sorting out the books and cleaning up the year end close. Her colleagues mocked her: she was going into a filthy snake-pit. Within three months, the accountant was running the business: she knew exactly where all the skeletons were, what could be cut and where some limited investment would make sense. She had converted a tedious administrative job into something which went straight to the heart of the business.

The power of the pen
As a young political researcher, I found myself in a room full of famous businesspeople and politicians who were going to draw up a new industrial and economic policy for the party. They all said profound and important things. I was out of my depth. So I said I would take the notes and draft up a discussion document for the next meeting. By accident, I had taken control. The next meeting

was anchored around my position paper. As long as the draft had a paragraph which reflected at least one comment from each grandee, they would be happy. All their other comments tended to cancel each other out: I was left as the only apparently impartial person in the room, because I was the mere note-taker. My industrial and economic policy was duly passed, and the political party duly imploded.

power meetings

For some, meetings are a wonderful alternative to real work. For others, meetings are the events where power is created or destroyed. In the words of Pierre-Francois, a senior French civil servant: "Meetings are a wonderful opportunity to destroy other ministries' agendas."

Take Pierre-Francois' view to heart when you next go to a meeting. If you go to a meeting hoping to get a decision made in your favour, be prepared to be disappointed. Meetings should never be used to make decisions. They can, however, be very useful in giving public endorsement to agreements you have reached in private with key players round the table. The Japanese call this process "nemawashi": building consensus before the meeting actually occurs. Even if there is one person who remains opposed to you, the process of nemawashi will have ensured that the majority is in support and you will know what the opposition looks like and how to deal with it. You will be set up to win.

From a PQ perspective, a successful meeting will have three elements:

- Control your agenda
- Make a contribution
- Make some allies

Control your agenda

If you are chairing the meeting, chair it. Do not let the meeting wander and ramble down interesting back roads. Do not let the meeting get sidetracked: that is a sign of weakness. You will gain more respect by keeping the meeting focused, keeping contributions focused and keeping to time. You will also achieve more by driving the meeting to action: make sure each agenda item is resolved.

Statistically, you are more likely not to be the chairperson. Even so, you should remain in control of your agenda. When you go to a meeting you should have a clear idea of what you want to achieve in that meeting: if you are not sure you can achieve anything at the meeting, do not go. Do not become one of the faces that turns up to meetings (to gain visibility or some other half-baked reason for attending) but never contributes. You will rapidly be recognised as a marginal player: at best, you will be a bag carrier or hanger-on for a real player. That is not the path to power.

Even if you are not the chairperson, you should still have your own agenda for the meeting which will have two major elements:

- Making a contribution
- Making some allies

These are discussed fully below.

Make a contribution

Next time you are in a big meeting, observe how the conversation flows. In many meetings the discussion takes the form of a series of dialogues with the chairperson. Most people shut up on most subjects. This is based on a common ground rule of meetings: the turf wars rule.

The turf wars rule is about respecting territory: "I will not attack your territory (agenda) if you do not attack my territory (agenda)." When the rule is broken, the victim will often retaliate later and viciously.

The turf wars rule means that you have to think carefully about where you will intervene. Even an honest and open question can be construed as a subversive attack on someone else. The one area you should want to make a contribution on is on the agenda item which relates to your territory. You do not want an open discussion on your agenda item. You want the meeting to be the public confirmation of the agreements you have reached in private with the chairperson and other key players, as outlined above. A strong contribution is one which results in something different happening after the meeting: a weak contribution is one where you simply share information but there is no action resulting from the information. That is likely to be an opportunity missed. When you have the opportunity to gain public endorsement, use it to drive action.

Death, paradise and territory

It was easy to spot the boss. Chief John was in his full regalia. He was wearing magnificent Bird of Paradise feathers in his head-dress which made him seem about three metres tall. I interviewed him about what it meant to be a chief of a traditional society in Papua New Guinea. I asked him what the most important thing is for his tribe. Without hesitating he answered, "Our territory. No territory, no food, no village. Territory is everything."

I then made the mistake of asking what would happen if I tried to take a square metre of his territory for myself. Chief John grabbed his spear and fixed me with his eyes. "Then I will kill you", he said. And he meant it. I quickly changed the subject.

If someone attacks your territory in a meeting, defend your territory so strongly that they decide to find a softer target elsewhere.

Make some allies

Often the most important part of a meeting happens round the edges of the formal meeting: while it is about to start, during a coffee break or just after it has finished. This is often the best time to meet someone who is normally hard to get to, to sort out any last minute issues or problems which may have cropped up. You should prepare for these informal meetings. Do not expect to resolve everything while you drink your coffee: you will probably be interrupted by other people wanting to discuss vital topics such as golf. But you should be able to flag your agenda item up and agree to meet separately and later. This is enough to control and accelerate your agenda.

The informal part of the meeting is also the chance to cement some alliances and do some intelligence gathering. A little flattery goes far: prepare in advance something nice to say to and about each person. Then ask them what is going on in their territory. Most of the time it will not be hugely relevant to you; occasionally you will hit gold dust. Again, do not expect to achieve everything over coffee: simply show your interest and agree to follow up later in private.

power presentations

Presentations can make or break managers, and managers know it. This sort of pressure does not help managers perform at their best. Consequently, it is relatively easy to stand out from your peer group, given that the average standard of management presentation is somewhere between abysmal and atrocious. There are no great secrets to presenting well: you probably already know what a good presentation looks like and how to prepare one. What follows is a simple guide to letting you achieve your true potential in presentations.

> **the average standard of management presentation is somewhere between abysmal and atrocious**

First, try a simple exercise.

- Step one: recall the three best presentations you attended in the last year. What do you remember most about each one?
- Step two: remember the three worst presentations you attended last year. What do you remember most about each one?

The chances are that you can not remember all the detail. You will probably remember something about how the presenter looked and sounded. And you may remember one or two really big messages that came out of the presentation.

Both the best and the worst presentations are dominated largely by style and appearance with the substance being dominated by a few key points.

Now think about how you prepare for a big presentation.

- How much time is spent wordsmithing the document, preparing appendices and working through all the detail?
- How much time is spent on rehearsing, making sure you appear well and on ensuring that one or two key messages really hit home?

The chances are that most of the time and effort is devoted to the detail which will not be remembered, but little time is spent on rehearsing and making sure that you make a real impact.

An effective presentation is a mix of good style and good substance. It pays to prepare for both.

Presentation style

You do not need to be a great orator to present well. You probably are already a good presenter, even if you do not realise it. To discover your innate presentation ability, try the following exercise:

- Do a presentation to describe the cost allocation system in your business. If you fall asleep before your audience, you have not succeeded
- Now do a talk on the most exciting (legal and decent) event that you have been part of in the last year

As you talk about something that has really excited you, you will probably start adopting the critical three E's of presentation style success:

- Energy
- Enthusiasm
- Excitement

The three E's are infectious: if you are energised, enthused and excited about a topic, you have a chance of making other people feel energised, enthused and excited about it. Put it the other way: if you have no energy, enthusiasm and excitement you can not expect anyone else to feel energised, enthused and excited on your behalf.

Now let's return to the challenge of presenting your cost allocation system: how can anyone demonstrate the three E's about that? To solve this riddle, we first need to jump into the substance of the presentation.

Making cost allocation systems exciting: how to build the substance of a presentation

Before preparing the substance of your exciting presentation about cost allocation systems, you need to answer three simple questions:

- Who wants to know about this? If you are presenting to fifty people, all with different perspectives and interests, you could land up with a buffet presentation: lots of different ideas all bundled up into one thirty minute slot. Nothing will be covered in depth; it will be difficult to establish either a theme or a clear and compelling message. Simplify things. Target the one or two people in the room who matter to you most: focus your presentation on those people
- Why do they want to know about this? Answer this, and you will be able to focus your presentation, identify a couple of clear messages you need to communicate and establish a consistent theme. The people you are targeting will be highly engaged; even the rest of the audience will enjoy a presentation with clarity, focus and purpose
- What do you want to achieve by the end of the presentation? Be clear about what will be different at the end of the presentation. Again, this is helps achieve clarity and focus

Once you have achieved clarity and focus, you will find a vast amount of the detail you were preparing simply disappears. You should be in a position to apply the 10–20–30 rule of presentations:

- Ten slides maximum. This is all you need to tell a story. If you are addicted to producing 300 slides, throw the rest in an appendix

- Twenty point typeface minimum. Don't read your slides: the audience can read faster than you can talk. The principle is to have simple slides and a smart presenter, not the other way round. Have simple slides which you bring to life with your explanations and insight
- Thirty minutes maximum talking. Concentrating for this long on one subject and one speaker is very difficult: energy and engagement levels drop the longer you speak. In a world where the pace of everything is accelerating, Attention Deficit Disorder has become endemic among managers. Don't fight against nature

You are now in a position to prepare a simple story. Unless you are doing a training event, most people will not want to know about the details of your cost allocation system, but they will want to hear a story. Any good story has three elements:

1. A beginning: "This is the challenge, problem or opportunity which our cost allocation system creates for us today."
2. A middle: "This is the journey we are going to embark on to do something about it."
3. An end: "And this is why we will all be better off (live happily ever after) once we have completed the journey."

You can be creative and state the destination (the ending) immediately after the start so that your audience have a context for understanding your journey.

Once you have a simple, compelling story focused on the right people you will find that you are not distracted or bogged down by all the detail. You will start to feel greater confidence about the presentation and your enthusiasm, excitement and energy will rise. Your style and substance will set you apart from your peers.

Clearly, there are many more tips and techniques for becoming a great presenter. Perhaps the most important is practice. Prepare and practice each presentation in advance. Even a two minute slot where you do no more than introduce someone else is a chance to shine: work to find the right words, the right tone. Practice also means doing as many presentations as possible: the more of them you do, the better you will become, provided you are trying to learn and improve all the time.

influencing and persuading people

The essence of PQ is making things happen through other people. You have to persuade them, sell them on your idea and your agenda. As a junior person with little authority, your selling and influencing skills are vital to survival and success. The more senior you become, the more of a salesperson you become. You spend less time actually doing things yourself, and more time persuading colleagues, clients and stakeholders to do things or agree things.

When people think of salespeople, they tend to think of them putting their foot in the door and trying to persuade hapless home owners to buy double glazing, encyclopaedias or eternal salvation. This would not be a successful way of selling in the C-suite. More subtlety and finesse is required. Ideally, they should not even think you are selling to them: you want to create the impression you are helping solve a problem for them. You want to be seen as their partner, not as a salesperson. This means moving from a win/lose mentality ("I will negotiate to win against you and you will lose") to moving to a win/win mentality. This requires seeing the world through their eyes.

There is a logic flow to all persuasive conversations, which can take from seconds (agreeing to go out for the evening) to years (selling a fleet of aircraft to a government). The logic flow of the conversation is the same in each case. Remember this logic flow and apply it when you need to persuade a colleague to agree with you or do something for you.

The conversation flow is as follows:

1 Agree the problem or opportunity
2 Agree the benefits of addressing the problem or opportunity

3 Suggest the idea
4 Explain how it works
5 Pre-empt objections
6 Reinforce the benefits
7 Close

If seven steps are too many to remember immediately, start with these three:

1 Agree the problem or opportunity (and why we should address it)
2 Suggest the solution and how it works
3 Close

As you follow this logic flow, remember the two ears and one mouth secret: listen twice as much as you talk. Selling and influencing is not about learning a salesperson's sales pitch, however convincing the patter may be. This logic flow also presumes you have done enough building of trust and mutual respect that both parties are ready to start a substantive conversation. If you have not reached this stage, follow the relationship and trust building ideas in sections 2 and 3.

1 Agree the problem or opportunity: interests versus positions

If you have a problem to solve, remember that you have the problem. The person you are talking to may or may not have the same problem: they certainly have a number of other problems which will be more important than yours. This means the starting point is not your problem: it is their problem. See the world through their eyes. This is where you have to be good at listening. If you talk at the other person, you will never discover what is on their mind. Let them talk. As they talk, take care to listen not just to their position but also to their real interests. There is a world of

remember the two ears and one mouth secret: listen twice as much as you talk

difference between the two. Often the response to a stated position will be the opposite of the response to their true interests, as illustrated in Table 4.1.

Table 4.1 Stated position and true interests

Stated position	Implied interest	Response to position	Possible response to interest
Cut your budget	Improve overall profitability	Cut your marketing spend	Grow profitable revenues: spend more on marketing
Reduce price of supplier's components	Reduce overall cost of production	Negotiate on price with supplier	Work with supplier to produce more reliable parts which lower overall production costs
All new products must be put through test market first	Reduce market risks: Product, channel, customer and competition	Test and pilot all new product ideas	Go straight from research to launch with good ideas to prevent risk of competition going to market first

2 Agree the benefits of addressing the problem or opportunity

Again, the trick here is to discover and express the benefits from the perspective of the other person. It may be very clear to you why you want your work put to the head of their in tray: what is the benefit to them?

About 70% of the effort and the time spent persuading will be spent on these first two steps. Once you have agreement on the benefits of solving a problem, they will be ready to move rapidly through the rest of the conversation. Do not move until you have secured this agreement.

3 Suggest the idea

This is the quickest part of the conversation. It may be just one sentence long. If they look horrified, go back to the start again: you have probably not got the problem agreed. If they are in total agreement and want to move ahead, skip the rest of the conversation and go straight to the close. If you carry on selling to someone who already wants to buy, you run the risk of saying too much and unselling your idea.

4 Explain how it works

Avoid too much detail. Focus only on those aspects of the idea which are relevant to the person you are talking to. As you do this, you can also cover the next two stages of the process: pre-empting objections and reinforcing the benefits.

5 Pre-empt objections

If you have listened well earlier, you will know what concerns the other person has. Avoid getting into a big debate about their concerns: this can quickly become a negative and unproductive discussion. The best way to deal with the concerns is to raise them yourself (this shows you have listened and respect their position, so they will trust you more) and then dispose of the concerns. Show that they can be dealt with.

6 Reinforce the benefits

By the time you get to this stage, the other person should be more or less ready to say yes. Quickly reinforcing the wonderful benefits which you jointly agreed early sets them up to say "yes" for sure. It is a more positive way of moving to "yes" than finishing on the negatives implied by dealing with objections.

If at any stage in the process you run into serious objections, do not get into an argument. Go back to the start and see if you can agree the problem and the benefits of solving the problem. You know you have laid the foundations well when the other person starts solving problems with you, rather than raising problems and objections for you to overcome.

7 Close

This is perhaps the most important part of the conversation, and it is frequently missed, with catastrophic results: all your good work is undone because nothing happens. People are not mind readers: you need to tell them what you want. You need to close the conversation by securing their agreement. There are four classic types of close:

1. The direct close: "Do you want to buy this computer?" Dangerous, because it invites them to think and, possibly, reply, "No". Then you are sunk
2. The alternate close: "Would you prefer the desk top or lap top version?" This is sneaky but effective. You are not giving them the choice of saying, "I don't want a computer". Many people meekly accept one of the two options given to them
3. The action close: "I will take the computer out to your car while you settle up at the cash desk." It takes quite a strong executive to resist the action close and say, "No you won't"
4. The assumed close: "Thank you so much for your custom. I am sure you will enjoy this computer. Let me take it to the cash desk for you." This is closely related to the action close, and is equally hard to resist

Persuading the traffic master to let you go speeding

We have already met Caroline, the account executive. She did a great job building a relationship with the much abused traffic master in the advertising agency. With his help, she stood a chance of getting her work scheduled promptly with the creative groups, the art department, media and all the other teams she relied on. He was the gatekeeper with the key to progress.

One day, Caroline was in a real fix. A client had seen some recent work and did not like it. The client asked her to rework: given copy dates were looming with the print media, the work needed to be done in a rush. She needed the traffic master to speed her work through the system.

The traffic master's position was pretty clear: there was no spare capacity and work had to be booked at least 72 hours in advance. That was standard procedure. Caroline knew that this position was merely a symptom of his deeper interests: he wanted a stable and predictable workflow so that neither the client teams nor the service teams would shout at him too much. Knowing this, Caroline had always been careful to avoid too many last minute requests. This meant the traffic master treated her last minute requests more sympathetically than the requests from other client executives which were always made at the last minute. She also offered to push back some other client work so that the overall load on the traffic master would not rise. Her last minute request sailed through, much to the irritation of more senior and more aggressive client managers who thought their work should come first.

By understanding the traffic master's interests (problem) she was able to negotiate a last minute request which conflicted with his normal position.

overcoming resistance

In theory, organisations should be models of cooperation, not conflict. In theory, there should not be wars, starvation and poverty. In the meantime, we have to live with reality. Colleagues will occasionally sabotage our plans, either by active resistance or by passively doing nothing when we need their help. If managers are to make things happen, they have to be able to deal with resistance.

By this stage, you will not be surprised to discover that resistance comes in three flavours:

- Rational
- Political
- Emotional

When you encounter resistance, you need to understand what flavour of resistance you are meeting, and to deal with it appropriately. Recognising the flavour is difficult because managers always pretend that their resistance is rational.

Rational resistance and responses

The first challenge is to know if someone is trying to stop you, or is asking questions for the sake of understanding and clarity. A few vital signs of resistance being disguised as questions are:

- Persistent questioning: beyond three questions about your idea, start to get worried
- Questions without solutions: if someone is supportive, they will not only ask questions but will also volunteer possible solutions, or will be supportive of the answers you give

- Continued focus on risks and problems, not on the upside of your idea
- The "yes but" game. This has several versions
  - "Yes I agree, but..."
  - "Your idea is wonderful, but..."
  - "You are doing a great job, but..."

Remember that everything before the "but" is bull: ignore it and focus on what they said after the "but".

everything before the "but" is bull

A rational response to a rational question is fine. A rational response to non-rational resistance is also common and useless. Most resistance is not rational. The one question you should ask yourself when you encounter resistance is, "Why is this person resisting?" Once you have answered the "why" question, all the other questions become relatively straightforward.

Perhaps the most common source of apparently rational resistance comes from staff departments: finance, health and safety, IT and HR. Some of their questions are rational and they can be helpful. But much of the time they simply want to know that you are paying respect to them by jumping through the hoops of fire, procedures and policies they have created and which they guard jealously. There is no point in arguing with them. Pay your respects to them early, make them feel valued, show that you are complying with their needs and they will mysteriously let go of minor infractions of their policies and procedures. Fail to pay respect, and you can expect a full frontal assault in which you are bound to have failed on some detail somewhere.

The value of reason and relationships

The Finance Department objected to the valuation of the business we had given to the board. Over the next few hours we found ourselves being challenged on the further reaches of finance theory and the capital asset pricing model:

- *Had we used forecast or historic risk premium data; how had we calculated it?*
- *What sort of beta had we used?*
- *How had we defined cash flow?*
- *How had we adjusted for discontinued operations and for acquisitions?*
- *How had we translated foreign earnings and minority interests?*

After a few hours of this barrage, we asked for an overnight ceasefire. As we thought about it, it was clear that their objections were nothing to do with how we had calculated the risk premium. Their real but unstated objections were:

- *We had not consulted them properly, so they wanted to take revenge for being sidelined in the valuation process*
- *We had given a low valuation which would embarrass them: they had told the board that the business in question was worth much more*

Instead of another pitched battle, we settled for dinner with the Finance Director. By the end of the week, we jointly produced a range of valuations reflecting different assumptions. The Finance Department saved face, and the board accepted the reality of the lower valuation.

Political resistance

If you present a threat to another department's territory, expect resistance. This resistance will never be presented as "get off my turf". Everyone is expected to pretend that they are team players working for the good of the whole organisation. They do not want to be seen to be acting in narrow self interest. All of their objections will be cast as rational objections to your idea.

As ever, the best way of dealing with resistance is to pre-empt it. You should know if you are about to step onto someone's turf. Approach them beforehand and see if there is a deal to be struck, if you can align agendas, if you can give them something back in return for their support. The simple act of reaching out to them early will help win their support. If they do not feel ignored and sidelined, they are less likely to resist.

Pre-emption is particularly important so that you can stop someone taking a public position against you. The moment someone takes a public position, it becomes very difficult for them to change that position. The pre-emption process should always be conducted in private. In private you are much more likely to hear their real concerns and you are much more likely to find a mutually acceptable outcome.

Once you reach the point of resistance, you have three options:

- *Power play*. Get a message sent from on high, from the CEO, that they need to fall in line. You will win the battle, but will lose key allies. No one likes losing and no one likes being outflanked
- *Alliance*. See if you can still do some sort of deal: find common ground, give them something so that they can declare victory (even if they have lost): let them save face
- *Surrender*: Some battles are simply not worth fighting. If you do withdraw, make sure you get something in return and stay in control. If you fight and lose, you become damaged goods politically

Conflicts, disasters and handicaps

We were working for the Air Traffic Control system. We found all sorts of quaint practices such as the "early off": this was a practice whereby a full shift of air traffic controllers would turn up for a shift even when only half were required. After an hour, half would be allowed to disappear and get their full day's pay. Many air traffic controllers have suspiciously low golf handicaps for people who work so hard.

As soon as we suggested some modest changes to these working practices, we were greeted with a chorus of shroud waving. They presented us with the inevitability that our changes would result in two jumbo jets colliding over central London, probably over Parliament during the state opening, thereby killing the entire royal family and political leadership of the nation. Naturally, their objections to reform had nothing to do with their desire to improve their golf handicaps even further.

There is no rational response to this. Shroud waving is used with equal effect when it comes to reforming health or welfare. Ultimately, this becomes a straightforward political question:

Are the benefits of reform worth the costs and risks?

Are we likely to win or lose?

Given these questions, the air traffic controllers were safe with their quaint practices.

Emotional resistance

The cult of macho management demands that people are always stretched to perform. Stretching people is generally a good thing: people tend to rise or fall to the level of expectations which have been set. If you want to make things happen you have to stretch people, and that is how they will learn and develop. But it is also possible to stretch people too far: to ask too much of them too soon. At this point, they break. When people break, all sorts of irrational and dysfunctional behaviour emerges: arguing over trivia, sabotage, unexplained absences, sudden illnesses. This often leads to the slippery slope of performance management: the oral warning followed by the written warning followed by dismissal and litigation for unfair dismissal, harassment and stress.

It pays to heed the warning signs. If someone is genuinely underperforming, then start the performance management process. But if someone is being overstretched, then do not attack them for resisting you: help them. The best way to help them is to take them all the way back into their comfort zone. This goes against the natural instinct of just letting off a little pressure to see how much stretch they can take. The nearest analogy is with mountain climbing: the remedy for altitude sickness is not to back down a few hundred metres. It is to go all the way back down so that the person can recover and acclimatise properly. With an over-stretched person, let them recover in their comfort zone, rebuild confidence and then slowly stretch to greater heights again.

PQ management is not about being aggressive: it is about being smart. In this case, helping is better than fighting. Recognise and use the cycle of performance in Figure 4.1. Push people out of their comfort zone into the stretch zone, but when they break down, take them back into their comfort zone for a while.

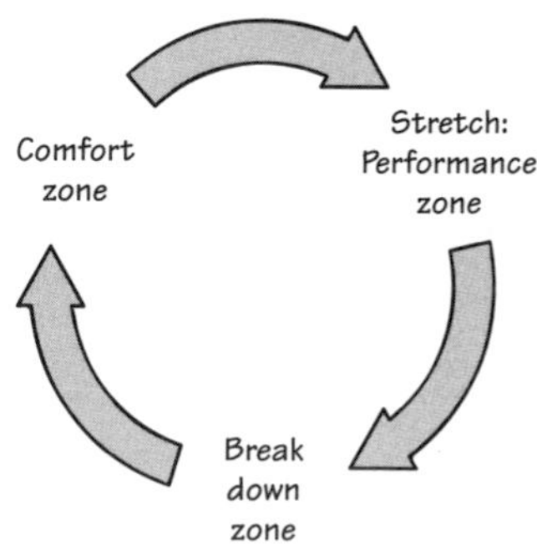

Figure 4.1 Leadership partnership

Ending resistance by giving support

It was 1am. Fifty executives had been struggling with the future of the company. They had finally recognised the severity of the challenge they faced: they had to transform or the company would go out of business. They also accepted that each of their business units needed to change radically. The problem was theirs and so was the solution. This was progress. I looked forward to making real progress the next day. I let them go to bed and promised to see them at breakfast at 7am.

At 1.15am Jan approached me in the corridor. He was a fifty year old company veteran. He had been one of the strongest opponents of radical change. He was now in tears, and he had not cried for thirty years. He knew that change needed to happen. He feared he could not make it; he just did not know how to do the things that were necessary. He felt that his career had been wasted and he had no future. He felt he had gone from being a valued executive to a worthless has-been in one day.

Ninety minutes later I had heard more about his career and life than was perhaps wise. He wanted reassurance and someone to speak to. He also desperately wanted to know that everything would somehow turn out alright: he had been pushed too far and needed to get back into the comfort zone. The next day we quietly worked out some simple first steps for him so he could rebuild confidence and start on what would be a difficult journey for him and his unit.

If you attack emotional resistance, expect increasingly irrational and violent reactions. Instead of attacking the person, support the person. Help them find a way through and an enemy will become an ally. A little listening can go a long way.

learning to say "no"

Saying "no" is essential: it is the way that you and the organisation can stay focused. For good reasons, however, being negative is not a good thing. Negative people are a drain on the energy and will of the organisation, and they are usually seen as poor team players. If you want to build power and respect, you have to find ways of saying "no" which are regarded as positive. There are three broad approaches:

- Do nothing
- The nice save
- The cheese shop game

Doing nothing is often the best PQ way of resisting the latest insane edict to be handed down from on high. As soon as you actively resist an idea, you have given it some legitimacy. By discussing the idea, you have made it a legitimate topic of discussion. This means the discussion will eventually be resolved. There are only two outcomes: you win the argument and lose allies by killing their idea. Alternatively, you lose the argument and you are seen to be a bad team player. By doing nothing, you put all the pressure on the other side to create some momentum and to justify themselves. They will find it very difficult to overcome the inertia of the organisation. If you see that the insane idea is going to become reality, you can still jump on board the bandwagon if you want to. If the idea dies, you will not be seen to be the assassin.

The nice save is best used on colleagues, suppliers and staff working for you. It should only occasionally be used on bosses. The principle of the nice save is simple: instead of finding all the negative sides of an idea, find the positives. Encourage your team

The principle of the nice save is simple: instead of finding all the negative sides of an idea, find the positives

member to build up the positive side of the idea, and quietly ignore the bad side of the idea. Focus on the positives makes them feel good even if they have to do extensive rework. Focus on the negatives simply invites conflict and argument. Even if you are right, you will have a demotivated partner.

The miracle of Daz and the nice save

The advertising agency was highly creative. Advertising Daz does not demand high creativity. Its basic message has not changed in fifty years: it is good for cleaning white clothes. Even the execution of the advertising has not changed much: we normally find a hapless housewife who is prepared to do the Daz test and say that she would not swap two packets of her old detergent for one packet of the wonders of Daz.

The agency arrived in Newcastle to pitch some new ideas. They were all insane. They were so bad that they were more or less guaranteed to win advertising industry awards while destroying the brand. But the reality was, we needed the help and support of the highly temperamental and highly strung creative team. So we needed to find a way of letting them down gently: we invented the art of the nice save.

Instead of throwing them and their ideas out of the office, we would find something good to say about each idea they came up with: we found ourselves having to be highly creative. Maybe the only good thing was that they had featured the brand prominently: we would get them to build up the positive aspects while downplaying the negative aspects. By focusing on what was good, not what was bad, we were able to have a half-way sensible conversation instead of a pitched battle.

The nice save is a subtle way of saying "no". Find all the good things about an idea and get the idea owner to build up that side of the idea. Ignore the rest: let it wither away. Slowly, they will turn a bad idea into a good one. Instead of feeling bad about rejection, they will feel positive about the feedback and will still own the idea.

The cheese shop game is best used on bosses. They will probably feel patronised if you try the nice save on them. They will feel offended if you say "no" to them. You need a way of resisting without being labelled a bad team player. Instead, you need to get creative: start thinking like the cult television show "Monty Python". One show had a sketch where a customer asked a cheese shop owner for a brand of cheese. The cheese shop owner had to find ways of saying he had no cheese, without admitting that he had no cheese. The excuses were many and varied (health risk, out of fashion, out of season, never on Fridays, etc.). Whoever runs out of cheeses to ask for or excuses for not having any, loses.

The managerial version of the cheese shop game is to find as many excuses for not doing something without actually refusing. There are several lines of attack:

- *Yes but*, as in: "Yes, that is a good idea but..." Now start identifying all the risks of the idea, and all the expensive and extensive requirements for success of the project which the boss will need to commit to if they are not to be embarrassed by failure
- *Priorities*, as in: "That is a good idea, just let me know how that fits with all the other really important things I am doing for you, and let me know which ones you want delayed"
- *The bait and switch*: understand the ultimate objective of the idea, and find either a better way of getting there, or someone else who is better suited to executing that idea

This is not a game you want to play too often with your boss. As ever, prevention is better than cure. The way to prevent yourself being asked to charge at windmills is to make sure that you have volunteered for, and are working on, sufficient important tasks that the boss dares not distract you with his or her latest hare-brained scheme.

crisis management

Crises are crucibles of experience which make or break managers. In our research on leadership, the top three qualities expected of a leader are:

- Vision
- Ability to motivate staff
- Ability to handle crises

If you want to gain and use power, you have to be able to deal with crises. There is one golden rule for crisis management: Don't avoid crises, control them. Successful crisis management is as much about how you behave as what you do. Stay calm, positive and action focused: let the others sink into arguing, denying and blaming and do not sink with them.

Don't avoid crises

Crises are inevitable. Things go wrong all the time. If you try to avoid crises, you will never learn from them. If you try avoiding crises, someone else will take control. They gain power, you lose power. It is better to try and fail early in your career than face your first big test later on. Experience really helps. After a while, you will notice that most crises follow a familiar pattern. It is the same pattern that Dr. Kubler-Ross discovered in people who are dying, which is the ultimate crisis we all must face:

1. Denial – "This can not be true"
2. Anger – "It can not be happening to me"
3. Bargaining – "Surely there must be a way of avoiding the inevitable"

4 Depression – "Ok, so this really is going to happen"

5 Acceptance – "Let's see what we can do about it"

Getting stuck in any of the first four phases above is a recipe for failure. You are not paid to go into denial and become angry and depressed, even although that is how you and your colleagues may feel. You are paid to move to action and find a resolution. If you are strong enough to do this, you will stand out from the crowd. Quietly, there will be many colleagues who are very grateful that you have saved them from a lot of pain. You will have marked yourself out and built significant PQ by not trying to avoid the crisis.

Profiting from crises

The claims department was the grubby underside of the insurance company. The glamorous part of the business was the revenue generating side: dealing with brokers, advertising and setting up direct channels. Occasionally there were cost cutting campaigns devoted to sorting out the company's overheads, but profits remained stubbornly elusive.

A quick examination of the insurer's books showed that over 90% of their costs were claims, which had never been actively managed. A claim is an expensive administrative chore to an insurer: it is a mini-crisis to the claimant. Closer examination found that the faster the claims agents settled a claim, the lower the cost of the claim. We pushed the logic all the way. After a while, most claims were settled immediately over the phone; car accident claims were often settled at the accident site. In each case the claimant would be delighted that the insurance company was taking care of the crisis and giving great service. They were happy to settle for modest amounts. The most expensive cases were always the ones which dragged on.

Since then, fast settlement of claims (and claimants' crises) has become an industry standard. This is not because the insurance industry is devoted to good service: they are devoted to minimising the cost of claims.

As with insurance crises, so with management crises: the earlier you can find a resolution, the less the pain will be. Don't avoid the crisis: deal with it.

Control the crisis

The best way to deal with a crisis is to prevent it. That is not always possible. Each crisis unfolds in its own unique and messy way. Typical crises will involve events such as a falling out with a major customer, key staff members threatening to leave and operational crises such as logistics or computer failures. As the crisis unfolds, it pays to work with a few simple principles:

- Recognise the crisis early
- Buy time
- Focus on outcomes

Recognise the crisis early. Don't hide from the offended stakeholder. See them early. Let them vent their anger and spleen: it is hard for people to maintain anger for long. Don't argue with them. Quietly make sure you understand their perspective and provide reassurance that you will provide the solution. You have now put yourself in control: you understand the stakeholder and the stakeholder is looking to you personally for the solution. You will either resolve the crisis yourself or find people who can do it for you.

Buy time. Don't make rash promises. If the solution is not to hand, do not bluster. This is the stage at which it is more important to ask good questions than it is to try and make up answers when you don't really understand the problem. As you talk with different people you will not just be finding out the problem, you will probably also be finding potential solutions and potential allies for delivering the solution.

Focus on outcomes. Crises encourage dysfunctional behaviour: people start playing the blame game, using analysis as a substitute for action, looking backwards not forwards. If you consistently look forwards, search for solutions and drive to action you will stand apart from most others. Avoid blaming anyone for anything, even if one person is to blame. If there is blame, focus on the system not on the person. You will be a role model and a safe person for others to confide in. You are also likely to be the person who resolves the crisis and your stock in the organisation will rise fast.

dealing with awkward people

Everyone is awkward at some point: even reasonable people get into conflicts and crises. To manage people is to discover human nature: everyone thinks that they are special and deserve special treatment. Everyone deserves the biggest bonus, the only promotion and the best assignment. As a test ask yourself and your colleagues whether they are below or above average in terms of:

- Ability to drive a car
- Parenting
- Making love
- Dealing with people
- Integrity

About 90% of people believe they are above average. This is statistically impossible, but emotionally inevitable. Anyone with self-respect does not see themselves as a below average human being.

Beyond the natural foibles of humanity and specific events which make even the most balanced person into a troublemaker, there are some people who seem to be awkward all the time. You may even have to land up working for such a person. Your task is not to change the person: you are a manager, not a shrink. Your job is to make things happen despite the behaviour of the person. This means you have to deal with their behaviour: do not worry about what events in their childhood may or may not have caused the behaviour. Focus on outcomes, not on analysis of their psyche.

90% of people believe they are above average. This is statistically impossible, but emotionally inevitable

For the sake of simplification, we will settle on three sorts of behaviour:

- Passive
- Assertive
- Aggressive

The ideal behaviour for a PQ manager is assertive: much dysfunctional behaviour is passive or assertive. Table 4.2 is a quick guide to each style:

Table 4.2 Three styles of behaviour

	Passive	**Assertive**	**Aggressive**
Relationships	I always lose – it's not fair or my fault	Win/win	I win you lose
Speech	Quiet	Open, conversational	Loud, talks over others
Group behaviour	Withdraws	Participates	Dominates
Crises	Shrinks	Future focus: move to action	Blames
Discussions	Agrees despite own feelings	Makes points clearly	Demands: my way or no way
How they make others feel	Guilty or superior	Valued and respected	Humiliated or angry and vengeful

Management TV shows, and many business autobiographies, endorse aggressive behaviour as a sign of strength and power. But creating an organisation full of humiliated, angry and vengeful people is not a great way to live or to make things happen. At the other end of the scale, passive behaviour is a recipe for losing. The ideal balance is assertive behaviour, and to maintain that style with both aggressive and passive people.

Assertive behaviour means being able to stand up to the aggressive types. Typically, aggressive people will attack the weakest players: make sure you are not the weakest player. Standing up to bullies does not mean fighting them: it means sticking to assertive behaviour. Be open and clear about what you need and what you expect, stay calm and focused. Do not get dragged into their emotional games: stay on a rational agenda and remain resolutely positive and future focused. Normally they will see sense and moderate their aggressive behaviour. Occasionally, they will become increasingly angry that they can not get their own way: let them make fools of themselves in front of everyone else while you remain calm and positive. Do not sink to their level: both of you will lose.

Passive behaviour is more common than it should be in organisations. It is not very helpful. These are the people who hide behind procedures and policies to explain why they can not do anything; they prefer the safety of analysis to the risk of action; they find excuses for failure. Do not try to make these people do things they can not do. Use them where their limited will and skill can best be used: they may be able to help in background support areas doing unglamorous and undemanding donkey work. This has the huge benefit of freeing up other talent to work on more demanding activities. Again, do not get caught in their emotional game of creating guilt trips for everyone. Be clear about what you expect and when you expect it, and make sure that they do not have the opportunity for shedding responsibility (and blame) back onto you or anyone else.

what: pulling the levers of power

It is no use acquiring power if you do not know how to use it. John Major, the former British Prime Minister, was accused of "being in office, but not in power". He did not survive in power much longer either. When you finally get your hands on the levers of power, you have to use them. If you don't use the levers, someone else will. With power, you use it or lose it. The more you use it well, the more power you will attract. Power attracts power.

Managing budgets, staff and reward systems are obvious sources of formal power. Controlling knowledge, projects and change are also formal sources of power. Money and budgets are sufficiently important to merit extra weight in this section:

- Negotiating budgets and the psychological contract
- Controlling budgets to deliver performance
- Managing budgets to make things happen
- Rewards and measures
- Staffing and structures
- Knowledge and power in the knowledge economy
- Projects management

Money: budgets and power

The currency of success is money, power and fame. In organisations, there is precious little fame to be achieved, except for the CEO hell-bent on getting their (normally his) picture into every newsletter, annual report and web page like a pumped-up despot of a small country. For most people, this leaves money and power as the real currency of success. This currency is hard earned and needs to be invested wisely if it is not to be lost.

Within the organisation, money comes as budgets. Budgets give power. Budgets help managers make things happen. Use the budget well to deliver great performance and you are on the way to earning more power. Use it poorly and you can expect to lose

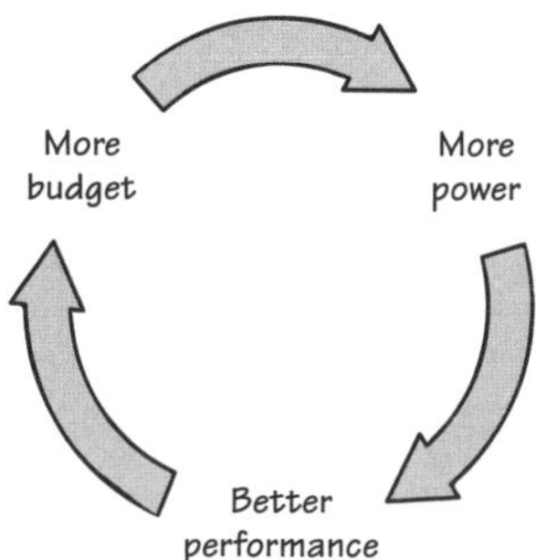

Figure 5.1 The virtuous circle of budgets, power and performance

both budget and power. As with much to do with power the motto is simple: use it or lose it. There is a virtuous circle which can become a vicious downwards spiral between budgets, power and performance:

There are three sides to using budgets well:

1 Negotiating the right budget
2 Controlling the budget
3 Managing your budget

The following sections look at each of these in more detail.

negotiating budgets and the psychological contract

Budgets are, in theory, the apotheosis of rational management. Budgets determine the best rational allocation of scarce resource in organisations. The only problem with this theory is that it is rubbish. Anyone who has worked in an organisation and has been capable of fogging a mirror knows that the budget process is not rational: it is intensely political. This is the point at which managers discover that the real competition is not in the market place: the enemy is within. Budgets are the battleground where managers compete with each other for scarce resource.

The best predictor of next year's budget is this year's budget

Next year's budget is the product of two main forces:

- *Last year's budget.* The best predictor of next year's budget is this year's budget, plus or minus a bit. Forget the story of thinking through priorities thoroughly. Most organisations are victims of their history. They simply continue on their existing trajectory and existing budgets with minor shifts trumpeted as major changes
- *Managers' negotiating skills.* The budget is not just a budget: it is a psychological contract between senior and junior managers. The junior managers bid for maximum resource and promise minimum performance in return; senior managers ask for maximum performance and offer minimum budget in return. This is a debate in which data is used not to find the truth, but to provide ammunition for each side's position. It pays to know how to manage this debate

If a manager is to make things happen, it is critical that they negotiate the right budget. Five simple principles help deliver a good outcome:

1 *Start early*. Before the formal budget process starts, anchor the discussion around numbers you feel comfortable with (see section 4). Most budget debates are about fine tuning some assumptions made very early, often by senior management or a planning group. If you get the right assumptions in place (about market growth, costs, prices, competition) then you are likely to get the right budget agreement
2 *Start high*. This refers both to who you start with and what you demand. When you anchor the discussion, make sure you anchor it with the key players from the Financial Director onwards. And pitch for more than you need: you know anything you ask for will be cut back, so ask for more. You may be cut back to what you needed in the first place
3 *Build your case*. Build an overwhelming case of data. You know more about your department or business than anyone else, so use that knowledge. You are not trying to present an objective case. You are pleading your case like a lawyer, so prepare your data like a lawyer: it will be one sided and on your side. Faced with an onslaught of data, most staff and planning groups will quietly give up and hunt easier and less well prepared corporate prey
4 *Build support*. Use your network to build support for your position. Make sure that the informal word on the network is supportive of you. Attempt to bring the staff and planning people on board. Use your coach or mentor to find out how the politics are playing out and how you can best position yourself. Create alliances with other departments where you have common interests: if IT wants to invest heavily, then make your budget dependent on that investment. IT will then support you, and if they do not get the investment you can renegotiate your budget as well

5 *Play hard*. The budget process is one of attrition. Naïve managers will accept a stretching target and then have a year of hell trying to achieve the impossible. For nearly achieving the impossible, they will miss out on bonus because they missed targets. Seasoned managers will spend one month playing hard ball to get a good budget, and then have eleven months of moderate work to beat a moderate target. They get the bonus not for one year of moderate work, but because of one month of hard bargaining

controlling budgets to deliver performance

Controlling budgets well is one of the basics of management. If you want to lose power fast, three of the quickest ways to do it are:

- *Miss budget*: even worse is to miss budget without warning. If things look bad, renegotiate your budget early. You will get beaten up a little, but not as badly as if you plain miss budget. Surprises are never good
- *Produce inaccurate budget data*. If you produce even one bad budget number, immediately all your numbers will be called into question and you will lose the trust and confidence of others. I have seen one successful CEO nearly get fired for this mistake: the board simply could not trust him or his numbers despite great operating performance
- *Not know your budget position*. Managers have to know all their key operating data and ratios by heart. A simple trick for venture capitalists is to ask applicants for a few basic financial ratios: surprising numbers of people fall at this very low hurdle

Controlling budgets successfully involves some basic strategies:

Hide budget. If you have planned your budget properly, you will know where you have overestimated costs, where you have planned cost savings which you have not told anyone about and where there is fat in the budget. This is your hidden contingency reserve. Keep it and hide it from the prying eyes of the finance department. You will more or less certainly need your contingency to deal with the unpleasant surprises that always turn up in the year.

Use the barbell approach to discretionary spending. Your discretionary budget is likely to be small. Spend it wisely. The barbell approach means spending some of it very early in the year, before it can be taken away by the finance department to make up for a shortfall elsewhere in the business. If you have an internal conference you really want to host, do it early. Keep the rest of the discretionary budget for the end of the year so that you can recover from the inevitable year end panic. If your budget does not get squeezed in the panic, you have the pleasant problem of spending your discretionary budget fast.

Prepare for the year end squeeze. Keep your eye on the overall corporate position. This will tell you how tough the year end will be: typically, you will be asked to deliver more profit (which means cut costs if you only have two months left in the year) and deliver more cash (reduce receivables and stocks, increase payables).

Do not manage cash or costs so tightly during the year that you have nothing left to deal with the year end squeeze that the finance department will inevitably produce.

Plan your budget on the 48/52 principle. Attempt to deliver 52% of the results with 48% of the budget in the first half of the year. If you succeed, the second half is easy. Even if you come up slightly short, this is less of a problem than coming up short against a 50/50 budget split.

managing budgets to make things happen

Once you have your budget, you need to use it well. The most important need is to meet or beat your budget target. The only question is how you use your budget to achieve this. There are two different approaches:

- Input focus
- Outcome focus

Input focus

Input focus means managing costs very closely. Keep an eye on the use of paper clips and plastic coffee cups. There are some benefits to this high control approach:

- You will not overspend
- You will probably have a very tight audit trail, so you can answer any awkward questions
- You will demonstrate high compliance to process
- You will not get fired

Input focus is much beloved of government departments and other traditional machine bureaucracies like life insurance companies and global systems houses. For them, it is more important to remove risk and have a compliant process than it is to achieve outstanding results or to innovate greatly. As long as the process is good, they believe they are largely immune to criticism.

If you live in an input focus world, control budgets very tightly. Follow the rules in the section above. Give subordinates very low discretion over spending, have tight authorisation limits and monitor budgets and spending frequently and closely.

Outcome focus

The outcome focus world has a different perspective. There is still a need to control costs – that much never disappears. But controlling costs is not enough in an outcome focus world. In this world, you will be measured on the results you achieve. If you control your costs but fail to achieve great results, do not expect to be congratulated. Given the focus on results, budgets tend to be more dynamic. They will be subject to revision and refocus throughout the year. The outcome focus organisation applies the basic principles of capitalism: if something is working, do more of it (spend more); if it is not working, stop it (spend less or change it). This is pretty simple stuff which is natural if you work in an investment bank, but is alien to government departments which are subject to the whims of politicians, not the winds of competition.

Living in an outcome focus world may be more exciting, but it is also more demanding. In this world, you rely on people, not the process, to deliver outcomes. This requires motivating and persuading them to go above and beyond to deliver outstanding results: they will not be highly motivated if you are tightly controlling them, not trusting them and not delegating in a meaningful fashion to them. You have to learn to let go in a controlled manner so that they can perform to the top of their abilities.

The difference between the two worlds is seen most clearly in the ritual game playing they go through at the end of the year. In the input focus world departments may suddenly go into a spending frenzy for the last two months of the year. Even if the spending is pointless, they need to spend their budget. If they do not spend their budget, they will find they have a lower budget for the following year. In the outcome focus world, the behaviour is the opposite. The last two months are likely to see real and virtual spending cuts so that profit targets can be hit. If things are going very well, then they may quietly start sandbagging for next year: they will find ways of deferring contracts and invoices so that revenue recognition is delayed until the start of the next year: that makes next year's target far easier to hit.

Neither the input nor output focus models are universally correct: they only work in the right context. Decide what sort of approach works best in your context, and then act accordingly.

Playing to win *versus* playing to avoid losing

David thought he was an excellent manager because he managed everything down to the last paper clip. Everyone else thought he was a control freak. He kept his budget very tight and only allowed anyone to spend it in very small, tightly controlled increments. He constantly reviewed progress to make sure that the money was being well spent, and constantly checked and challenged what everyone was doing. Because we had to go back to him on more or less a weekly basis to get more budget, his control was complete.

Quickly, people learned to give David what he wanted. It might be great, it might be stupid. It did not matter. If you wanted to do anything, you did it his way or not at all. We all kept our noses clean and did the minimum required to avoid messing up. Trying to innovate was pointless. It was a compliance culture. But it worked. In the world of large scale systems integration the emphasis was on process compliance, risk minimisation and tight control. David got results and anyone who wanted a life got out.

John appeared never to ask much about budgets. Instead he discussed with us what we needed to achieve. We then talked about how long it might take and what sort of resources would be required. We were then left to get on with it: if we needed help we were expected to ask for it. If we messed up occasionally, that was OK provided we still achieved the end goal. In practice we knew that we were expected to over-deliver against our promises, innovate and come up with some contribution to the wider organisation. This was a very high commitment culture which probably suited the relatively free-wheeling spirit of strategy consulting.

Working for John was far harder than working for David. David would be happy if you did as you were told and did not mess up. John really expected something exceptional. In their different contexts, both were successful.

rewards and measures

"You only control what you measure and you only get what you reward" is an old adage which remains reasonably true. As a manager, your ability to reward (or punish) different sorts of behaviour and performance is very powerful. You can use rewards and measures to redirect performance.

two groups who are most rational in their decision making are economists and psychopaths

For instance, we found that one life insurance company was very successful at selling a range of products which were catastrophically unprofitable. Meanwhile, they were missing out on all the profitable product categories. A little further probing found the reason for this: the incentive schemes for the sales force were skewed in favour of the unprofitable products. Essentially, the salespeople were doing informal, personal calculations around how much time and effort it took to sell a product, how likely they were to succeed in selling each product and how much commission they would earn if they were successful. We then changed the incentive scheme radically in favour of the profitable products, and gave them training to help them succeed. The product mix of the company changed completely within twelve months.

That story should indicate the power of rational decision making. But most people are not wholly rational. Psychologists have found that the two groups who are most rational in their decision making are economists and psychopaths. Unless you employ a team of psychopathic economists, you will need to deal with emotion and politics as well. In the case of the apparently rational salespeople, we found we could mess with their incentive schemes, provided we did not mess with their cars. We decided to give a modest upgrade to all their cars. This was very powerful. Their friends, family and neighbours would not know how much the salesperson earned, but they would see what sort of car they drove. The car signalled their position in society and their relative success. Upgrading their cars bought us the right to mess with the rest of their compensation scheme.

Choosing the right rewards and measures is fraught with danger. A rational person will find the easiest way of achieving the best outcome. When politicians decided to start setting targets for the UK National Health Service, disaster was more or less bound to strike. Two examples:

Target: Cut the waiting time for operations.

Responses: Redefine the time from when the wait starts

Ask people on the waiting list to confirm their requirements within seven days; write to them during the vacation period. When they do not respond, remove them from the waiting list.

Target: End the practice of keeping patients on trolleys in public areas.

Responses: Remove the wheels from trolleys and redesignate them as beds

Reclassify lobby areas as wards.

At the end of the process, the targets had been met and nothing had improved for the hapless patients. Such game playing is rife. Look at how CEOs and Financial Directors manipulate accounting data to produce exactly the results (plus a bit) that the stock analysts are predicting. In extreme cases the results culture leads to outright deception: the demise of Barings came about when one rogue trader (Nick Leeson) who had a very good knowledge and control over the accounting systems in the Singapore office started circumnavigating all the corporate controls and making ever bigger and failing bets in the market place to make his numbers. He failed, and the whole bank went down with him.

There are three approaches to setting rewards and measures to make things happen, depending on the culture of the organisation:

- Rules based culture
- Principles based culture
- Mission and values based culture

Game playing will happen in each sort of culture, but you will achieve different sorts of performance in each culture.

Rules based culture

The rules based culture is typified, once again, by the machine bureaucracy. This appears to give managers high and increasing power. The more targets there are, the more the manager must be in control. In the limited sense of power being about control, then the rules based culture gives high power and high control. It does not necessarily give high performance: it creates a compliance culture of achieving the minimum rather than a commitment culture of overachieving. The natural tendency for a rules based culture is to create ever more rules and ever more inspections to ensure the rules are being achieved. GPs (UK Primary Health doctors) have contracts which spell out 76 clinical performance measures, 56 organisational performance measures and a few more measures besides. Their compensation is driven by how nearly they meet over 130 goals. No one can remember 130 goals, let alone perform to them in a meaningful way. Most people struggle to reconcile more than about three goals.

The Midas Touch: be careful what you wish for

King Midas had helped the Greek god Dionysus. Dionysus decided to grant King Midas a wish. Midas asked that anything he touched should turn to gold. Dionysus obliged and invited Midas to touch a stone and an oak leaf. The stone and the oak leaf turned to gold as soon as Midas touched them.

Midas was overjoyed. He told his servants to prepare a great feast to celebrate his good fortune. He sat down to the feast and picked up the food, which promptly turned to gold. Shocked, he picked up a goblet of wine to drink. The goblet turned to gold, and as soon as his lips touched the wine, the wine became like golden ice. Accidentally, he touched his daughter. She turned into a statue of pure gold.

Midas cursed his luck. He asked Dionysus to be released from the curse he had brought upon himself. Dionysus told him to jump into a nearby river. Immediately, the river turned to gold and Midas died, releasing him from his curse.

Principles based culture

A principles based culture will still have rules and will still have measures. But they will be much more broadly based than in the rules based culture. They will often include qualitative measures such as "client satisfaction", "initiative" and "teamwork". The principles based culture is common in professional service firms (lawyers, consultants, accountants); at senior levels in most organisations, and in organisations where performance is often about quality and other hard to define measures.

For instance, measuring the performance of an HR department is not easy. It is not a question of how many people were hired or fired: much of that will be driven by the operating units. Detailed measures such as the speed with which benefit policy enquiries were answered are largely useless: very simple game playing can pervert such measures. At minimum, they could play the call centre trick of answering all the calls quickly and badly. Normally, you need to come back to principles based measures which may be framed as simple questions:

- Are we developing and retaining our best people?
- Are we raising the quality bar in our recruitment?
- Are we managing our benefits policy fairly and cost effectively?
- Are we building the right sort of organisational culture?

Honest answers to these questions presumes a degree of trust which a rules based culture would not presume. If the trust is abused, then underperformance is more or less guaranteed. If the trust is well based, then a principles based approach is an invitation to innovation and overperformance which the rules based approach kills.

Mission and values based culture

At the opposite end from the rules based culture is the mission based culture. Even here, everything may be measured. But the measures are not regarded as ends in themselves: they are regarded as stepping stones towards a greater good. The voluntary sector is often mission led: goals for charities are often very broad such as "reducing inequality", "eliminating child poverty", and "alleviating hunger in developing nations". The mission for Teach First (a UK educational non-profit organisation) is typical: "to address educational disadvantage by recruiting exceptional graduates and transforming them into effective teachers and outstanding leaders in all fields". This is pretty broad brush as a measure, but it drives everything the organisation does. It will only recruit people who share its values and goals. It develops professional support programmes to help its participants succeed as leaders and as teachers. And it measures everything. Even if you turn up to do a talk for them for free, you will be measured and assessed. The purpose is not to reward the speaker (there is no reward anyway): the purpose is to see how much the intervention is helping Teach First achieve its mission. If it works, they will want to do more of it. If it did not work, they will change what they do. Measurement in a mission based organisation is more about learning and development and less about immediate rewards.

The PQ approach to rewards and measures

In practical terms, most managers have to live within the culture of their organisation and department. If you live within a rules based culture, play by the rules. Playing by the rules means manipulating the rules to your advantage so that you can always show that you have achieved the many measures you will be subject to. If you live in a principles or mission based culture, you should expect to have to overperform and overdeliver.

If you have discretion over how to set rewards and measures, then you have a choice to make.

- Rules based measures and rewards gives you high control and high power: it does not normally give you high performance
- Principles and mission based measures and rewards require more trust and give you less day to day detailed control, but they are more likely to give you high performance

Rewards and measures are unusual for the PQ manager: power and performance pull in opposite directions. The more daily power you exert over the details of the process, the more you constrain the possibility of either underperformance or overperformance.

staffing and structures

Fifty years ago, C Northcote Parkinson laid down an immutable law of organisational life: "An official wants to multiply subordinates, not rivals" (*Parkinson's Law*, John Murray, 1958). This was based on observing that as the British Empire declined, the number of officials in the Colonial Office rose. There was an inverse relationship between the number of staff and the amount of work (if any).

For many managers today, the number of staff they control is still a vital sign of their self-importance. From a PQ perspective, this is a mistake. The ability to make things happen does not come from the number of people you have. It comes from the quality of the people and your ability to control them. For example, if you are given the option of running a call centre with 800 people in Bangalore, or running the planning department of eight people at corporate headquarters, it is clear where the real power lies. The 800 call centre staff may be more useful to the customer, but the eight people in planning have more power. The eight people in planning can eliminate the 800 in Bangalore with greater ease than the 800 in Bangalore can eliminate the eight planners in head office. Power is not just about numbers.

The first stage is to make sure you have the right people in your team. Performance between a top performer and a low performer is often vast. For instance, in developing a bank for small businesses we found that the best relationship managers were typically three to five times better than those in the bottom quartile of performance. Since most banks paid bonuses up to 25%, this gave us a great opportunity: we could poach all the best relationship managers by doubling their salaries and achieve far superior performance as a result.

Be ruthless in acquiring the best talent. You have three ways of acquiring the best talent:

Identify and woo the best talent internally. HR systems may flag up good people, but more often word of mouth and reputation will tell you most of what you need. Treat this as a long term seduction. It may take months of quiet flattery, enthusing them over what is happening in your area, showing that you care for them and building trust. This is an investment which pays off hugely once you have the people on your team.

Play hard ball. Refuse to accept people onto your team who do not meet your needs. Inevitably, HR will be trying desperately to place the untried new talent and some talent that has been tried and found wanting. You should look hard at these people: often there is great untried talent, and there is often great talent that has failed because of lousy management. Be prepared to take on some of these people as part of a deal in which you also get the best people.

Deselect the people you do not want. If you are appointed to a new position, do not assume you have to live with the team you have inherited. Look at how often the bulk of the executive team changes within a year of a new CEO being appointed. You do not need to fire people: just by making them feel unwanted they will vote with their feet and you can help them find suitable positions elsewhere. This may seem cruel, and it is. Your loyalty is ultimately to the success of the organisation as whole, not to preserving people in jobs where they should not be. IBM and others have an explicit strategy of culling at least the bottom 10% of performers every year. Survival of the organisation takes precedence over survival of the individual.

Survival of the organisation takes precedence over survival of the individual

The trap that many managers fall into is filling positions because the position is vacant. Avoid this. Do not fill the vacancy until you are convinced that you have the right person for the job. Expect each person you hire to raise the quality bar in your unit. To recruit at speed is to repent at leisure.

Once you have the right people, you need to be able to control them. If you are surrounded by power barons, then you need to break their power and make them work to your agenda, not to theirs. The initial strategies for achieving control are:

- Building trust
- Creating a clear agenda for everyone to follow
- Putting in place clear rewards and measures
- Controlling key resources, especially budgets

Occasionally, you will also need to restructure to gain full control. See Joyce's story below for how this can be achieved.

Riding the corporate carousel

Joyce was appointed head of European Systems. She inherited a team which had done reasonably well. It was clear that they really did not want her for two main reasons: she was a woman, and she was American. She was not welcome in the European boys' club. It was a club in which each country was allowed to do its own thing and was dominated by some real power barons. Condescendingly, they explained to her how each country was different culturally and economically and needed a different approach.

After a month of hearing all these stories from the regional power barons, she realised that she was in danger of being in post, but not in power. In practice, all the power was held at country level. So she decided to reorganise around industry groups such as Financial Services, Government, TTT (Travel, Transport and Tourism) and others.

Junior managers heard about this and sighed cynically. They had seen it all before. Moving from geography to functional and industry grouping and then back to geography again. The corporate carousel keeps on turning until it finally reaches the point it started from. They wondered when the next reorganisation would come.

The junior managers missed the point. The reorganisation was not about strategy, although it helped to develop expertise and focus on multinationals and industry sectors. The real purpose of the reorganisation was to let Joyce gain control.

Amid howls of protest, she reorganised the top team. She fired a couple of the top managers in the process: public executions have a remarkable effect on behaviour.

intellectual arguments are merely servants of political positions

After the reorganisation, the power barons were cowed. They could no longer hide behind national boundaries. They had to learn new rules of the game: Joyce's. She had the particular pleasure of seeing how the top team which used to argue strongly against local interference, were now arguing strongly against the countries which were preventing cross-border cooperation in support of their industry groups. She discovered that intellectual arguments are merely servants of political positions.

knowledge and power in the knowledge economy

"Knowledge is power" is one of the most common beliefs about power. It is also a source of great confusion, because knowledge means different things to different people. Some people think of knowledge as information ("know what") or skills ("know how"). From the perspective of PQ, it is worth looking at three sorts of knowledge and how they can be used.

- Secret intelligence
- Political intelligence
- Asymmetric information

Of the three, political intelligence has the highest value and least risk to a high PQ manager.

Secret intelligence

Secret intelligence is nothing more than knowledge which someone does not want you to have. It is, to a large extent, the origin of the saying "knowledge is power". When the British broke the Enigma code in the Second World War, they had access to all the coded instructions to German U-boats: this was secret intelligence and because the British had it, they were able to win the Battle of the Atlantic with more than a little help from the USA. In America, J Edgar Hoover ran the FBI from 1923 until he died in 1972. Several presidents wanted to get rid of him, but he had amassed files of embarrassing data on many leading politicians. This was a form of secret intelligence which kept him in office well beyond his use-by date.

In the business world there is a subterranean industry devoted to corporate espionage. But for most practising managers, secret intelligence is not the high road to success. If you need to survive by blackmail, then something is wrong. There are easier ways of succeeding.

Political intelligence

Political intelligence may not be secret, but it can be hard to discover. In the business world political intelligence goes beyond the formal information systems to help people at all levels discover what is really going on in the organisation. It is the informal knowledge which most PQ managers trust more than the formal information.

Political intelligence will answer questions such as:

- Are the rumours of reorganisation true? What will happen, how will I be affected and what can I do about it?
- How does the promotions process really work and how can I improve my chances?
- What do I need to do to get the assignment I really want?
- Are the financial numbers coming out of division x really accurate? What is really going on there?
- What is the budget process for next year, and how can I influence it positively?
- What are the real risks behind this new business idea? What are they hiding from me and can I trust the proposal?

Clearly, this is the knowledge that people really value. It is one of the reasons managers gossip at the water cooler, and it is the reason they value corporate events. The training and the speeches may not be much use, but the chance to network and find out who is doing what and what is really happening is highly valued. This makes political intelligence the opposite of secret intelligence. Everyone tries to keep secret intelligence secret. Political intelligence is based on sharing intelligence as much as possible:

the broader and deeper your network the better your political intelligence will be. Be prepared to share your political intelligence with others: you need to be able to trade knowledge, not keep it secret.

find the intelligence behind the information

Even CEOs are in constant search of political intelligence. Essentially, they do not trust the information they are presented with every day, because they know the information is biased. Many of the apparently informal and *ad hoc* conversations they have each day help them find out what is really happening: they want to find the intelligence behind the information.

Intelligence in action

P&G deserves its reputation as a mighty marketing machine. It also used to be a gossip shop. All the brand assistants and brand managers were in deadly competition, not with Unilever (that was the easy bit of the work) but with each other. The trivial problem of internal competition involved resolving conflicts between competing brands. The really intense competition was about who would get promoted or fired. Much time was wasted in hushed conversations over the coffee machine, or slightly less hushed conversations in the pub, about who was up and who was out.

Marketing people tending to be both entrepreneurial and venal, they started a book on who would get the next promotion and who would get fired. With money at stake, this placed a premium on gathering inside information. Over time, the book achieved unerring predictive accuracy, much to the annoyance of both senior management and of HR. The rest of us found the book very useful: it was an extremely candid assessment of where we stood in the performance stakes. It was much more honest than the evasive and sugar-coated formal assessment system.

The odds quoted in the book were the product of classic intelligence gathering. We observed how everyone was performing closely, and how senior management interacted with each person; we made friends with everyone connected to the promotions process; we stayed

close to the head hunters: they often had very good inside information about who was looking for jobs elsewhere and who was doing very well. There was no single source of information, but the collective information gathering and analysis of the whole department proved very accurate.

Of course, if we had spent as much time, effort and ingenuity on gathering intelligence on our market place and external competitors, we might have performed even better.

Asymmetric information

Asymmetric information is a basic building block of most negotiations. Typically, neither the buyer nor the seller want to reveal their limits, constraints, margins or options. This is as true within the organisation as it is beyond the organisation. Standard operating procedure is to make sure that the Finance Department does not know how much fat there is in your budget for this year or in your proposed budget for next year. You should know more about your business than they do, and this should enable you to pad the budget. Naturally, the Finance Department will work hard to overcome this information deficit so that they can remove the fat and redeploy your money where they think it can be used better.

Asymmetric information is a soft form of secret intelligence. It needs to be treated with caution inside an organisation. In the short term, you can win budget battles and proposals by hiding information and spinning all the other information to your best advantage. In the longer term, this has the effect of making you untrustworthy. Other managers, especially your bosses, will learn to distrust any numbers you present to them. You will then have to work twice as hard to persuade them of your case, and to rebuild lost trust.

Everyone expects that there will be some game playing and using of information to advantage. Play the game too hard and you lose credibility.

project management

Successful managers often learn their trade and start to shine by executing projects successfully. Early in their career the projects may be small. By the time they reach the C-suite the projects can be as big as leading a major merger integration programme. Projects test and develop managers. They involve the fundamental task of making things happen, even when you do not have all the formal authority to make it happen.

Typical project management courses focus on the technical detail of running a project well. It is worth knowing some of this, but they do not make a project succeed or fail. Success and failure is based on how well you manage the three dimensions of change:

- Rational – IQ
- Political – PQ
- Emotional – EQ

If you need someone to run the technical side of the project, there are plenty of technical project managers available in the market place at relatively low cost. In terms of making things happen, the technical side of project management is the least important. An effective PQ manager will focus not only on the technicalities of the project, but also on the political and emotional aspects of the whole change. The project is the technical side of the broader change agenda.

Projecting irrelevance

Ed was very happy. He had just been appointed project manager for a major start up. He had been trained as a project manager and knew what would be required. This was his chance to shine. The start up was going to be particularly challenging because it was a joint venture between three different organisations. He realised that he had the pivotal position: he was the one neutral, competent manager who could pull all the different parties and priorities together. If he did it really well, they might even make him CEO.

Ed set to work. He interviewed everyone and started to produce a risk log and an issue log, together with potential remedial actions for over 200 risks and issues he had identified. He liaised with lawyers on the technical detail of setting up the company where he found many more issues, questions and problems. He produced timelines in the form of PERT and GANTT charts which showed that because of the seasonal nature of the business we were in huge danger of losing a whole year. He identified many of the differences between the three partners which could derail the whole programme. He mastered the project.

He had also made himself completely irrelevant, so we fired him.

The management team knew that there were lots of risks, issues and differences between the partners. They knew there was time pressure. They knew if they stopped to worry about all of that, they would never achieve anything and would land up arguing with each other. Instead of focusing on problems and analysis, they focused on solutions and action. The pace was very high, and the politics were inevitably intense. The politics tended to move six steps faster than the project manager could keep up with: he was recording last week's problems which had been solved and was unaware of this week's problems which we had learned to hide from him.

Under huge pressure, the start up proved to be a big success. Without being expert project managers, the leadership team had managed the project well by:

- *Focusing on solutions and action, not on problems and analysis*
- *Actively managing the politics and the people*
- *Dealing with the big issues, not getting sidetracked by the detail*

To make things happen in a project, you need to deal successfully with the rational, emotional and political aspects of change.

Rational project management

Rational project management normally focuses on the details of risk management and creating a time line for the project based on a critical path analysis. That is important and worthy, and there are plenty of technicians you can hire to do that job for you. From a PQ perspective, you need to focus on a much bigger and simpler question:

> "Are we solving the right problem?"

Put simply, the right answer to the wrong question is wrong. The answer "Canberra" is fine if the question is "What is the capital of Australia?" It is useless if the question is "How do we reduce our costs by 15%?" Knowing what the right question is begs one more question: "How do I know if I am answering the right question?" Here are three simple tests:

- Where's the pain? The project is sustainable if there is real pain or opportunity attached to it. Normally, this can be expressed as a money value: launching this product on time will make us $5 million, or cutting these costs will save us $10 million. Opportunities which have no measurable value, such as changing culture or creating a knowledge base are often exciting: they are also the projects which are most likely to run out of steam or get cut at the first sign of trouble. If you can put a credible money value on the project, it is more likely to succeed
- Who's feeling the pain? CEO projects never fail: they get all the support, staffing and funding to make them succeed. Even if they do not do too well, history is rewritten to show that they succeeded (provided the CEO remains in post). Conversely, mid level managers and their projects find it much harder to gain the right level of support and funding. Mid level managers are also dispensable: they are allowed to fail. Make sure that the project is anchored with the most senior person possible. This also gives you visibility and profile when the project succeeds

- When will the pain become intolerable? Urgent projects always beat important but long term projects. Long term projects can be delayed (until they become short term and urgent). Short term projects can not be delayed

If you are working for the CEO on a project with big and immediate financial implications you will have more profile, support and better chances of success than if you are working for a mid level manager on a long term project with no quantifiable financial benefits. This is obvious. Despite this, most people land up working on the wrong sort of project: frustration tends to be the main outcome of such projects. Working on the right project accelerates your career: you succeed fast or fail fast.

Working on the right project accelerates your career: you succeed fast or fail fast

Political project management

From a PQ perspective, answer three questions before embarking on a project.

1 Do I have the right project sponsor?

2 Have I got the right team?

3 Have I got the right position on the project?

Each of these three questions is answered below.

1 Do I have the right project sponsor?

This dovetails with the rational question of "Who is feeling the pain?" The most senior person feeling the pain should be the sponsor of the project. The sponsor should not be involved day to day. The role of the sponsor is to:

- Call the project into being
- Ensure it is staffed and funded properly
- Oversee progress on a regular but occasional basis
- Help overcome roadblocks on the way
- Determine when the project is finished

If the person you think is the sponsor is unable or unwilling to do all of the above, find another sponsor or another project.

2 Have I got the right team?

If you get the A team, mountains will become molehills and you will achieve great things. If you get the B team, molehills will become mountains and you will not sleep for the duration of the project. The team should have a good mix of:

- Technical and functional skills
- Access to all the right stakeholders in the organisation
- Individuals with strong interpersonal and political skills

You know you have the right quality of team member if you are told that your choices are all too busy and too important to be released onto your project. Those are exactly the people you want. If you can not get them released onto your project, your political early warning radar system should start signalling approaching danger. Either your sponsor is too weak to broker the necessary deals, or your project simply does not have the priority and importance you thought it had.

Inevitably, you will be under pressure to take on a few people who are not A team players. If you have managed your network well, you should know of some new and untested talent that you believe is very promising, and you should know of some talent that has had a hard time simply because they were on the wrong project with the wrong boss before. Pick a few of those and then you can play hardball on insisting that the rest of the team has to be established A team players.

3 Have I got the right position on the project?

All projects involve a mixture of grunt work and glamour. You will know you have the right position on the project (which does not always have to be in the lead role) when you are sure that:

- You will enjoy the work and the people you will work with
- You will learn and develop, as well as contribute your skills
- You will gain recognition and visibility for your contribution

This raises the inevitable question: "How do I find such a position?" The best answer to this, and to many other aspects of successful management is: "Start early".

Your network should alert you to exciting projects and death star projects which are on the horizon. When you see a death star project looming, do a Harry Potter: wear the cloak of invisibility. Suddenly become very busy on lots of other projects and start volunteering for things so that you are indispensable. When you see an exciting project, throw the cloak of invisibility away. Make yourself useful to the potential project early, using some of your discretionary time. The earlier you become involved, the more you are able to shape the project the right way and to position yourself for the right role. By the time the project is formally announced, you are too late: the major decisions have been made and the staffing has been largely decided. You will be left to pick up the crumbs, at best.

Emotional project management

"Emotional" is not a word which is usually associated with project management. Now think of the late nights, the crises, the conflicts and arguments, the passive and aggressive resistance you encounter, the frustration, stress and tension leading up to a key deadline. Emotion can rip through a project like ice ripped through the "Titanic": silent, unseen and deadly.

Challenges such as crises and conflicts are dealt with in section 4. From a project perspective, the critical insight is to understand that all projects follow a predictable emotional roller-coaster. There are typically six stages in the roller-coaster:

1 *Enthusiastic start*: by the time you start, everyone should recognise the need to change and want to change. You normally start on a high

2 *Initial sprint*: in many well managed projects, there are some early wins and early signs of success. These are important because they help silence the critics and bring the doubters on board: everyone wants to join a successful bandwagon

the reward for succeeding in a project is another project

3 *Into the valley of death*: slowly you discover all the opposition to your plans, all the complications and obstacles in the way of progress and all the risks and issues you feared. A fast start slows down into a struggle through the swamp

4 *Rock bottom*: there is a moment when you realise that it can get no worse. Do not try to avoid this near death experience: it is cathartic. This is the moment when people realise that the current way of doing things is simply no longer possible: we have to move on, we have to make progress. At this point, people stop clinging to the past and can start building for the future

5 *Long hard climb back up*: the climb may be hard and long, but it is positive. The team and the organisation should now be looking forwards and moving to solutions and action, instead of looking back and doing analysis to find more problems. Enthusiasm for the project should now be reviving

6 *Successful finish*: this is often forgotten: projects need to be closed rather than being allowed to drift on. And the reward for succeeding in a project is another project: you get to start all over again

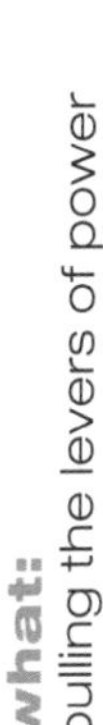

The best way to ride the roller-coaster is to sit tight. Do not try to get off and stop it or redirect it: you will get seriously injured. Give people the time and the space to go through this emotional cycle and recognise it for what it is. Often opposition to a project is temporary: you will have moved further and faster along the change cycle than people who are not on the project. Give them time to catch up; be sympathetic to their concerns but do not be

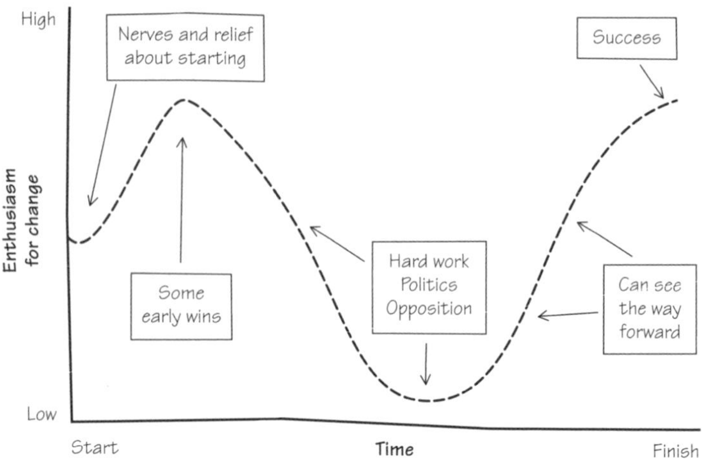

Figure 5.2 The change cycle
Source: Leadership Partnership [logo]

derailed by them. Do not try to argue rationally with emotional concerns. Fighting emotion with reason is like fighting fire with fuel: not a good idea.

Riding the roller-coaster of change

Linda knew she had a problem. She was the head teacher and she was going to have to shut the entire school down permanently within 18 months. Shut down is not good for any workforce. But for teachers, who are used to a high degree of job security, this was disaster. A new school would open nearby, and she could guarantee that they would all have a job, of some sort, at the new school. But the new school would have new governors, new direction, new values, new methods, new management. Nothing would be the same. It was not clear whether any of the staff would be willing or able to make the transition to the new school.

Linda had tried talking to the staff. She had tried listening to the staff. Nothing worked. She was aware that there was a huge rumour mill going on in the staff-room. None of the rumours assumed that good things might happen. Linda knew she needed to create an open and honest dialogue if she was to bring the staff with her to the new school.

In an act of mild desperation, Linda created a huge wall chart with the "Change and valley of death" roller-coaster on it (Figure 5.2). She hung it in the staff-room and explained it to staff. The floodgates opened. Suddenly, the staff realised it was OK to feel bad about things, and that they could talk about it and discuss it openly. They all started to track where they were on the roller-coaster; they even started competing to see who could reach the valley of death first.

There were still many hurdles for Linda and the team to jump. But by legitimising the emotional roller-coaster everyone was riding, it became possible to have a sensible dialogue about what needed to happen. Most of the staff rode the roller-coaster successfully into the new school.

why: use it or lose it

For many people, the purpose of developing PQ skills is simple: it is to gain power and to enjoy the trappings of power and wealth. At its extreme it takes the form of senior executives awarding themselves more or less guaranteed bonuses, re-pricing their option schemes and creating ever more lavish pension and benefits programmes for themselves while slashing costs and jobs for the ordinary worker. In its gentler form it can be seen in partners who are quietly serving out their time, and taking more than they contribute, or with senior executives using their position as a platform for networking at the opera, and with prestigious charities, commissions and committees. This sort of life is very attractive, especially if you have spent twenty years working for it. It is also an abuse of responsibility; it corrodes morale and trust across the organisation and is a huge missed opportunity.

PQ skills can be self-serving, but they are also fundamentally about making things happen. Power is pointless unless it is put to good use. As a leader, you need to make things happen. In Kissinger's words, a good leader is someone who "takes people where they would not have got to by themselves". In other words, simply being a steward and letting the organisation run its natural course is not leadership. You have to make a positive difference if you want to be a successful leader.

"takes people where they would not have got to by themselves"

In this section we look at what happens when you finally arrive in a position of real authority and how that authority can be used effectively or abused. The sections are:

- The delusions and reality of power
- Agenda power
- The art of unreasonable management
- Knowing which battles to fight

the delusions and reality of power

Something odd happens when you finally become partner or CEO. Suddenly, all your jokes become funnier. Your taste in art, food and wine becomes excellent. Your judgement and ideas become better. At least, this is how people behave to your face. Instead of stifling a yawn at your feeble attempt at a joke, they chuckle merrily. Instead of quietly taking you to one side to tell you when you are being daft they treat you like the fountain of all wisdom. When you have an idea, you may be alarmed to find that people have gone away and acted on it, even though it was no more than a passing thought. This power can go to people's heads. They can start believing that they really are as good as all their courtiers pretend. They conveniently ignore the reality: the courtiers are being nice to them because they want a piece of their time, resources and authority. Senior leaders find that they have no neutral, objective discussions: everyone is after something from them.

In this heady atmosphere, leaders often fall into one of two common traps:

- Activity *versus* achievement
- Position *versus* performance

Although senior executives fall into these traps most often, managers at all levels are capable of falling into them. Use this section as a health check and to make sure you avoid these common traps.

Activity *versus* achievement

Try this simple test. See how many presidents of the United States, or leaders of your country, since the Second World War you can name. Once you have named them, see what you remember them for. The chances are that you will remember them for at most one or two things: in the case of presidents from Nixon to Clinton, they probably will not be remembered the way they want to be remembered.

Next, see how many past CEOs of your business you can name, and what they will be remembered for. Again, they will probably only be remembered for one or two things at most.

Finally, what will you be remembered for?

Let's look at some of the things you will not be remembered for:

- writing approximately 100,000 separate emails in a career
- making 100,000 phone calls
- attending 10,000 meetings
- working late at the office
- meeting budget in 2008
- getting a good bonus in 2018

Like the many presidents and prime ministers who work very hard, you will not be remembered for any of that. You will be lucky to be remembered for one or two things at most.

To make this test a little easier: how will you remember this year in twenty years' time? What do you remember from twenty years ago? If that is too difficult, try ten years or five years ago. Again, the chances are that you will remember each year for one or two things. There are some years which I find difficult to recall at all: the only thing I seemed to achieve was to get one year closer to death. That is a waste of a year.

If you do not have a clear agenda and clear goals, you will drift. You can not achieve goals you do not have. This goes straight back to one of the key principles of PQ: you must have a clear agenda to gain and use power well (see section 2)

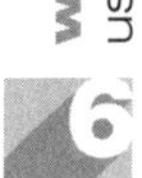

Position *versus* performance

Here is another simple test. You are at a social event and someone asks you what you do. What do you tell them?

When I ask this of people, the common reply is something like, "I am the Vice President/Director/Partner/Big Banana of Mega Corp". They are not saying what they do. They are describing their position and asserting their self-importance. At one level this is a harmless social convention. But it often also betrays a confusion that people have between position and performance. They think that seniority is an endorsement of their success, and if they are successful they must be performing well. At this point, it is worth remembering that the career expectancy of a new CEO is now under five years and falling.

The reality is we all live in a performance culture. There is no escape. The more senior you become, the more you have to perform. To make things more difficult, you have to learn new rules of the game at each level. What made you a successful junior auditor will not make you a successful CEO. The skills and expectations are simply different.

Once again, the antidote to this trap is a clear agenda. If you know what you want to achieve you are likely to be performance focused rather than indulging in the entitlements of rank.

agenda power

Perhaps the best book you never need read was written by Jack Welch, the former chairman of GE. It is called *Control Your Destiny or Someone Else Will*. Once you have read the title, you do not need to read anything else: you have read the most important message of the book. The rest is detail.

If you have any responsibility in an organisation, you have the chance to shape the agenda in your area. If you do not create the agenda, someone else will create it for you. It may not be the agenda you want. If you control your agenda, you control your destiny.

A good agenda is a vision without the hype. You do not need to be like Martin Luther King declaring, "I have a dream..." If you have dreams in the office, keep them to yourself. A good agenda is much simpler. A basic agenda is like a story in three parts:

- Here is where we are
- This is where we are going
- This is how we are going to get there

A really great agenda adds one more element of magic:

- And this is the important role you will play in helping us get there

You do not need the oratorical skills of Churchill or King to tell such a simple story. But if you do it well, you will not only win control of the rational agenda: you will also win control of the political agenda and win hearts and minds. You will be at risk of being seen as a good, even great, leader.

Telling stories

The start up: professionalisation
The start up had been a great success, built on the dynamism and initiative of a few great staff. It was also, to be truthful, something of a shambles: it was a mixture of inspiration and perspiration with no real preparation. The CEO decided that the story he wanted to build was simple: "professionalisation". He pursued this agenda relentlessly. It meant putting in proper finance and accounting systems; stabilising the operations; building an IT system which actually worked. It also meant replacing 90% of the staff over two years: entrepreneurial people do not like stable and predictable systems. At the end of two years, he had a sustainable organisation rather than an unsustainable band of enthusiasts.

Japan: integrating into the global business
The Japan business was dead in the water. This should not have mattered much, except that I was running it. I built a simple story. We would invest in making this a successful and integrated part of the global business. This would be cheaper and better than buying a new company and hoping to integrate that one. And internally, this gave us the focus about what sorts of clients we should sell to (global clients) with what sorts of products (global products) and even what sort of training we should do (global, not local). By selling the story of "investment" I successfully reclassified predicted losses in the business (a Bad Thing) as investment (a Good Thing). Stories are deceptively powerful.

School: building a culture of respect
The head teacher decided, with the staff, to build a culture of respect in the school: this was to counter declining standards of dress, behaviour and performance. Respect was the first, essential building block towards success. The staff thought this was a great idea. Then they discovered that this meant they had to start dressing properly for school; it meant that they had to keep their classrooms looking immaculate; it meant that they had to return all homework properly marked within 24 hours of it being submitted. Once you build a story, you can push it a long way.

To build a successful story, you need to do two things:

- Strike early
- Collaborate

Striking early means you need to publish your story before someone else writes and publishes the story, your agenda, for you. Once your agenda has been written for you, you have lost control.

There is no point in publishing your agenda or story if no one believes it or accepts it. So you need to work fast to build buy in to and acceptance of your idea. Often, the best time to build support for your story is before you have formally declared your agenda. This allows you to consult with key constituencies and ask for their advice around a number of options: if you are smart, you will position two or three options so that everyone gravitates towards the option you prefer anyway. You are then able to declare that you have taken and will follow their great advice: no one opposes an idea if they think it is their own.

> **no one opposes an idea if they think it is their own**

You have to get the story right. If you build the right story, it focuses effort and discussion. Each element of the story needs to be right:

- Here is where we are
- This is where we are going
- This is how we are going to get there
- And this is the important role you will play in helping us get there

Let's look at how each element can be built to succeed.

Here is where we are

This is where you paint a picture of the challenge that needs to be addressed. You will know you have a worthwhile challenge if other people are feeling pain as a result of this issue.

If the only person losing sleep is yourself, tough. If several of your bosses are losing sleep over the problem, you have probably found a worthwhile challenge. In power terms, you will get plenty more support for a shared problem with high profile rather than a problem which is purely within your own department. Once you are tackling the big problem, you normally find that you can sort out your local problems in the context of the bigger problem.

There are plenty of long term problems. We should probably all do more about our pensions, climate change and world hunger. But today the problem is called getting into work, sorting out childcare and dealing with tax. Immediate problems always take priority over long term problems.

Here is where we are going

The start of the story is the challenge; the end of the story is the happy ending. You need to show people that you are taking them to a better place than they are in today. You need to make this relevant to each constituency. For instance, in the Japan story (above and below) the story was about becoming a profitable part of the global network. To which the legitimate response is, "So what do I care?" You need to make an abstract statement relevant and compelling. For each key constituency, this is how the message translated:

- Shareholders: this is the low cost way to profits compared to buying a new business in Japan
- Global industry heads within the firm: this is how we will grow a business for you which can support your clients consistently and effectively
- To local staff: this is how we will secure your jobs in Japan, and give you opportunities across the globe

This is how we will get there

This links the start and the end of the story. It is perhaps the most important piece of the story because this describes what you will do differently from the past. Think of this as your theme tune. You will keep on playing it, relentlessly, so that every time anyone sees you they automatically think of your theme tune. This makes it very easy to:

- Focus effort and discussion
- Decide what you should do
- Decide what you should not do

This theme tune needs to be very simple. Not many people remember a ten point plan. Your agenda may be both important and very subtle to you, but you are going to have a very limited share of mind from most of your colleagues. They will remember one, at most two, things that are important to you. Make sure they remember what you want them to remember. A theme tune can be thought of as one of those prize draws where contestants have to complete the following sentence in not more than twelve words: "Next year we will…" Examples of successful entries into the theme tune competition include, "Next year we will:

- Reduce our costs
- Professionalise our organisation
- Refocus on our core competencies
- Build customer service
- Create a culture of respect"

These are simple and memorable themes which can be reduced to slogans unless they are backed up by action.

I first learned the importance of focus in gaining customers' share of mind when I became Mr Daz. My first task as manager for Daz was to watch fifty years of advertising for the brand. In fifty years, the core message has not changed: Daz is good for white clothes. This is not subtle, and it undersells all the other myriad benefits of Daz. But shoppers have many other things to think about and worry about besides the technical marvels of Daz: if we can get remembered for one thing, we have succeeded.

This is how you can help us get there

Organisational life is not a spectator sport: everyone has a part to play. This means you need to tell a story in which your colleagues have a clear role to play. If you fail to do this, they will simply become interested but passive listeners to your tale. In the example of the school (above and below) the head teacher asked staff to be the role models for the new respect agenda. This meant:

- High standards of personal dress and hygiene
- Always handing back homework fully marked within 24 hours of it being submitted
- Role model appropriate behaviour in the class room

Only after the staff had become good role models could they start enforcing the respect agenda on the students. A zero tolerance approach on uniforms or tardiness would not be credible if the staff were shabby and late themselves.

Putting it all together

The essence of a good story is simplicity and brevity. This is very hard to achieve. In the words of Winston Churchill, at the end of a long letter to his wife Clementine: "I am sorry I wrote you such a long letter, I did not have time to write a short one." Verbosity is the enemy of clarity. Making things simple requires very clear thinking.

Once you have achieved clarity, do not be afraid of constant repetition. As a rule of thumb, do not expect people to hear, believe and act on what you are saying until you have said it to them five times. To make the point, here is the essence of a good story for only the third time: since you bought this book you must be smart enough to pick things up quickly:

- Here is where we are
- This is where we are going
- This is how we are going to get there
- And this is the important role you will play in helping us get there

The essence of the story can be captured in a very few words. Table 6.1 is a translation of the three stories outlined earlier, but now put into the framework of an effective story. In each case a very simple story was able to drive and focus the organisation for two years:

Table 6.1 The framework of an effective story

	The start up	**Japan**	**School**
Here is where we are	Enthusiastic, highly stressed, unsustainable success	A local business losing money, going bust	Standards and achievement are slipping
This is where we are going	Stable, sustainable success	Profitable part of the global network	Firm foundations of success
This is how we will get there	Professionalising everything we do	Integrate, collaborate with global business	Build a culture of respect
This is what it means to staff	Change or move	Global training and work experience; retain a job	Improve dress, return homework, etc.

the art of unreasonable management

PQ managers know the limits of reason. Effective PQ managers are all selectively unreasonable. Consider the corporate battles in Table 6.2.

Table 6.2 Corporate battles

Traditional incumbent	Current challenger
Xerox	Canon
British Airways/American	Ryanair/Southwest Airlines
GM/Ford	Toyota/Honda
Hoover	Dyson
IBM (Lenovo)	Dell

The battles above are now well established battles between major rivals. Now turn the clock back. When Canon, Honda and Ryanair started out they had nothing in terms of traditional competitive advantage: they lacked the resources, skills, knowledge, budgets, distribution systems and brand strength of the incumbents. When Soichira Honda stood on his soapbox and said he was going to take on GM, any reasonable person would have told him he was nuts. GM had no idea who Honda was: they know now. Reasonable people do not build great empires or great businesses.

Reasonable people will listen to all the reasons why their dream will remain just that: a dream. They will never achieve their ambition. Reasonable CEOs listen to all the reasons the cost cuts can not be delivered, the innovation must be delayed and the profit forecast must be downgraded. They will not last long as a CEO.

Unreasonable managers do not listen to all the problems and all the excuses. They listen to the people who bring solutions and drive to action.

There are some unreasonable managers who are unreasonable about everything. They are painful to work for and with; they are often destructive of both people and businesses. There is an art to being successfully unreasonable. The main principles are:

- *Pick your battles*. If you fight on too many fronts, you spread your resources too far and lose on every front. Pick the few battles you must win, focus your resources and win those battles. Leave other battles to another day or to other people
- *Be inflexible about the goal, flexible about the means*. Achieving a stretching goal will require hard work and creativity. Do not presume to have a monopoly of wisdom: your team will probably have great ideas on how to get there. Let them take ownership over how they achieve the goal, but the goal remains constant
- *Be demanding but supportive of your team*. Remember there is a difference between being demanding and being demeaning. Bullying people does not get the best out of them. Set high standards, then help the team achieve them
- *Focus on action and solutions, not on analysis and problems*. Smart people are good at thinking. When thinking gets in the way of action, being smart is a serious handicap to leadership. Find a solution which works. Do not try to find the perfect solution: it does not exist

Do not try to find the perfect solution: it does not exist

knowing which battles to fight

There are two approaches you can take to fighting the inevitable corporate battles:

- The Nelson strategy
- The Sun Tsu strategy

The Nelson strategy

This is high risk and high reward. Admiral Nelson, perhaps the most successful naval commander in history, laid down a simple doctrine: "Any captain who lays his ship alongside that of the enemy can do no wrong." In other words, whenever you see the enemy, attack. In later years, Lord Cochrane followed this doctrine to an extreme. He was commanding a frigate (no more than a lightly armed reconnaissance ship) when he saw a full battleship. He launched what appeared to be a suicidal attack. He won.

This highly risky strategy has its merits. It awes the competition into submission. Soon enough, no one dares to take you on and you quickly start to get your own way on things. Under Nelson, the British kept all the enemy fleets in harbour for years: they simply did not dare to venture out. You learn to fight to the last drop of blood on everything. The more you fight, the better you become at fighting.

The downsides to this strategy are fairly obvious. First, you may lose. Second, even if you win you will also lose all your friends and allies.

This is a strategy which works for some types of people: entrepreneurs, successful naval commanders and psychopaths. For most managers, a slightly more subtle PQ approach is best.

The Sun Tsu strategy

Sun Tsu, the Chinese philosopher, wrote *The Art of War* approximately 2,400 years ago. He laid down three rules of warfare which are a good guide for most managers in dealing with corporate conflict. Think of some recent corporate battles you have been involved with, and check them against the three rules below:

1. *Only fight when there is a prize worth fighting for.* Many corporate battles suffer the bike shed problem: everyone argues over trivia like "What colour should we paint the bike shed?" It is easy to have an opinion on this and the subject is obvious. Meanwhile, the really important things such as "Which IT system should we use?" prompt little discussion outside IT. No one else understands the problem. Do not fight over the colour of the bike shed. Save your energy for the battles which really matter
2. *Only fight when you know you will win.* There is a saying on Wall Street: "If you don't know who the fall guy is, you are the fall guy." If you don't know you will win, you will probably lose. And most battles are won and lost before the first shot is fired: the side which has lined up the most support and picked the right battleground will win. Make sure you have the support and position to win
3. *Only fight when there is no other way of achieving your goal.* This raises the problem that the Nelson strategy faces: first, you may lose. Second, if you win the battle you will also win some enemies. It is better to find ways of avoiding a head-on collision. Find ways of changing the agenda, aligning interests, resolving differences in private. A public battle is never dignified

Most corporate battles fail at least one, and sometimes all three, of these tests.

conclusion

Managers live in a world where PQ is becoming ever more important. We can not rely on command and control. In a world where responsibility exceeds authority we have to develop a new set of skills to make things happen. Being smart (high IQ) and nice (EQ) is not enough. Successful managers now have high political skills (PQ). PQ is a series of learnable skills and behaviours: building alliances and networks, doing deals, building trust, dealing with conflicts and crises, negotiating and influencing.

PQ is an idea whose time has come. Organisations are essentially political creations: we all want to know who is in, up or out and where everyone stands in the pecking order. PQ is also the way that managers can make things happen: IQ and EQ are not enough to make the organisation work in your favour. PQ is essential to managerial survival and success. *Power at Work* is the first book to show what the new rules of survival and success mean for the practising manager.

PQ points the way to a new breed of manager succeeding. It is not enough to be a brain on sticks. Nor do you need to be an expert in psychological theory. You need instead to develop a deep understanding of how to make the organisation work for you. This is not all about the dark arts: it is about learning to use ambiguity, crises, conflict and all the other daily challenges of management life to your advantage. PQ requires learning how to win through other people, not against other people.

***Power at Work* is the first book to show what the new rules of survival and success mean for the practising manager**

Many old-fashioned managers feel threatened by the new world of change, uncertainty and opportunity. They prefer the old certainties of their command and control world. Their time is over, except in the old dinosaur organisations of machine bureaucracies such as government.

It is time for the old generation to step aside. A new generation of managers is taking over, exploiting new technologies, building new businesses and discovering new ways of managing. For the new generation, ambiguity is opportunity. Lack of resources and authority is not an obstacle to achievement. With PQ skills, managers learn to achieve far more than their formal resources or authority would seem to permit. PQ converts a world of ambiguity into a world of opportunity.

With PQ, a threatening world becomes an exciting world of achievement not constrained by the traditional limits of age, budgets and authority. The management journey may at times be uncomfortable, but it is likely to be exciting. But whatever your journey is, enjoy it.

appendix

Political environment assessment tool: scoring guide

This assesses how political your particular environment is. See table 1.2 and accompanying text to interpret your scores.

		1 Disagree strongly	2 Disagree slightly	3 Half-way	4 Agree slightly	5 Agree strongly
1	My responsibility exceeds my authority	1	2	3	4	5
2	Resources are allocated strategically and rationally	5	4	3	2	1
3	You get the resources you negotiate	1	2	3	4	5
4	My goals for this year are clear	5	4	3	2	1
5	My goals remain unchanged over the year	5	4	3	2	1
6	The promotion process is fair, rational and transparent	5	4	3	2	1
7	You need strong sponsorship to get promoted	1	2	3	4	5
8	Assignments balance the needs of the organisation and the individual	5	4	3	2	1

	1 Disagree strongly	2 Disagree slightly	3 Half-way	4 Agree slightly	5 Agree strongly
9 You get the assignment you negotiate	1	2	3	4	5
10 There are not enough promotions to go round	1	2	3	4	5
11 There are not enough bonuses to go round fairly	1	2	3	4	5
12 My boss frequently praises the team	5	4	3	2	1
13 Mistakes are used to help people learn and develop	5	4	3	2	1
14 Sort problems out before the boss finds out	1	2	3	4	5
15 The real rules of survival and success are not written down	1	2	3	4	5
16 We operate an up or out policy	1	2	3	4	5
17 This is a highly ethical and moral organisation	5	4	3	2	1
18 Honesty is highly valued	5	4	3	2	1
19 Politically astute people get promoted first	1	2	3	4	5
20 I trust my boss completely	5	4	3	2	1

Index